fireplace
Decorating & Planning Ideas

Better Homes and Gardens® Books
Des Moines, Iowa

Better Homes and Gardens® Books
An imprint of Meredith® Books

Fireplace Decorating & Planning Ideas
Editor: Paula Marshall
Writer: Judith Knuth
Associate Art Director: Mick Schnepf
Designer: David Jordan
Copy Chief: Catherine Hamrick
Copy and Production Editor: Terri Fredrickson
Book Production Managers: Pam Kvitne, Marjorie J. Schenkelberg
Contributing Copy Editor: Jennifer Mitchell
Technical Reviewer: John Emil
Contributing Proofreaders: Nancy Dietz, Sue Fetters, Joe Irwin
Contributing Illustrators and Designers: Carson Ode, Mead Design, The Art Factory
Indexer: Kathleen Poole
Electronic Production Coordinator: Paula Forest
Editorial and Design Assistants: Kaye Chabot, Mary Lee Gavin, Karen Schirm

Meredith® Books
Editor in Chief: James D. Blume
Design Director: Matt Strelecki
Managing Editor: Gregory H. Kayko
Executive Shelter Editor: Denise L. Caringer

Director, Retail Sales and Marketing: Terry Unsworth
Director, Sales, Special Markets: Rita McMullen
Director, Sales, Premiums: Michael A. Peterson
Director, Sales, Retail: Tom Wierzbicki
Director, Sales, Home & Garden Centers: Ray Wolf
Director, Book Marketing: Brad Elmitt
Director, Operations: George A. Susral
Director, Production: Douglas M. Johnston

Vice President, General Manager: Jamie L. Martin

Better Homes and Gardens® Magazine
Editor in Chief: Jean LemMon
Executive Building Editor: Joan McCloskey

Meredith Publishing Group
President, Publishing Group: Christopher M. Little
Vice President, Finance & Administration: Max Runciman

Meredith Corporation
Chairman and Chief Executive Officer: William T. Kerr

Chairman of the Executive Committee: E. T. Meredith III

All of us at Better Homes and Gardens® Books are dedicated to providing you with information and ideas to enhance your home. We welcome your comments and suggestions. Write to us at: Better Homes and Gardens® Books, Shelter Editorial Department, 1716 Locust St., Des Moines, IA 50309-3023.

Note to the Reader: Due to differing conditions, tools, and individual skills, Meredith Corporation assumes no responsibility for any damages, injuries suffered, or losses incurred as a result of following the information published in this book. Before beginning any project, review the instructions carefully, and if any doubts or questions remain, consult local experts or authorities. Because local codes and regulations vary greatly, you always should check with local authorities to ensure that your project complies with all applicable local codes and regulations. Always read and observe all of the safety precautions provided by any tool or equipment manufacturer, and follow all accepted safety procedures.

reflectyourstyle

FIREPLACES ARE CHAMELEON-LIKE, CHANGING character to reflect their surroundings. You determine the look of your fireplace with the objects you arrange on the mantel, the tools you place on the hearth, the chair you put beside it, the color you paint the wall that surrounds it.

On the stage set of your home, you are director and designer, playwright and stage manager. A fireplace can take the lead or play a supporting role in setting your room's style. If you have a fireplace you love, make it a focal point and write your room's design script around it. If your fireplace lacks star quality, read on for ideas about how to groom your lackluster performer for top billing.

In this book, you'll find fireplaces that tuck modestly into small spaces and bold fireplaces that command attention, fireplaces flanked by bookcases, surrounded by windows, and bracketed by benches.

Fireplaces have changed through the centuries, reflecting the tastes of various times and various regions. In this chapter, you'll find rooms that highlight a range of fireplace and fireside styles, starting with a massive old-world stone fireplace and ending with a sleek, contemporary steel-fronted hearth.

As you consider your fireside style, trust your instincts. Surround your fireplace with the colors that cheer you, the fabrics that comfort you, and the treasures that capture your past.

Polish your room's image with a fireside style that reflects your taste.

OldWorld

IN THE STATELY HOMES OF 17TH-CENTURY Europe, grand stone hearths provided welcome warmth and an enticing gathering spot for family. Still, it's a sure bet that any aristocrat would have gladly traded his imposing but inefficient fireplace for the comfort of a 20th-century thermostat.

Luckily, you can have the best of both worlds. To re-create the old-world fireside elegance of a French chateau or English country manor, think big. These fireplace openings, hearths, mantels, and surrounds are all weighty in appearance and large in comparison to other fireplace styles.

Check with architectural salvage firms for antique stone or marble fireplace surrounds or look into cast stone versions that mimic more expensive materials. Wood-paneled walls and ceilings and exposed beams contribute to the look of solidity. Floors of natural or simulated stone, slate, or large-scale tiles are a good choice, as is dark-stained wood flooring.

Warm the floors with richly colored area rugs. When choosing fireplace screens and tools, avoid refined finishes such as polished brass. Instead, opt for a dull pewter finish or the hefty look of wrought iron.

Finally, select deep, generously sized seating pieces and sturdy tables that are proportional to the scale of the fireplace.

The romance of fireplaces begins with the baronial stone splendors that created warmth in Europe's Middle Ages.

Look to the details for inspiration: The cove ceiling above the fireplace, *left,* repeats the curve of the stone surround. The scroll pillars on the fireplace surround are based on a detail found in the adjacent kitchen.

NewClassical

THE SINUOUS CURVES AND SUMPTUOUS FABRICS of Neoclassicism swept through the salons and sitting rooms of the fashion-conscious early in the 19th century. Inspired by Napoleonic conquests and British explorations, cabinetmakers and designers of that era produced furnishings steeped in the traditions of ancient Rome, Greece, and Egypt.

To bring this classic look to your home, choose a formal fireplace that combines refined materials and graceful proportions. Center a convex mirror over the fireplace, then dress the mantel with a symmetrical arrangement of classic objects such as vases or candlesticks. Select sofas, chairs, and daybeds with scrolled arms and backs. Favored fabric motifs include Roman eagles, Greek lyres, and stylized Egyptian lotuses.

This style, sometimes called Empire, was popular in the United States through the 1870s. You may be lucky enough to find exuberant antique or reproduction pieces with carved dolphins or winged sphinxes supporting marble tabletops. For a more restrained look, stencil a Greek-key design around the perimeter of the room just below the ceiling or use a similar design on the floor or in an area rug.

Ancient civilizations left a rich design vocabulary that continues to inspire furnishings and design.

Even without a fire, this fireplace exudes elegance, *right*. An armload of slender logs fills a brass container to create a striking still life in an unlit fireplace.

THE CABINETMAKERS OF 18TH-CENTURY America seemed to build the virtues of the budding republic right into their furniture. Queen Anne and Chippendale tables, chairs, and cupboards express a cordial dignity and strength of character in keeping with the times. Fireplaces also possessed the solid, dignified appearance.

Even if you don't have a period-style hearth, you can achieve a similar fireside feel by surrounding your fireplace with inviting seating. Pull up a pair of wingback chairs to your fireplace, and you've taken the first step to creating this ever-popular style. The winged sides and high backs of these chairs were originally added to protect the sitter from drafts; and these features remain popular because of the comfort they provide. Upholster the chairs in gleaming damask for a formal look; opt for leather or linen for a more casual versatility.

A brawny fireplace calls for large-scale accessories, such as a large painting above and heavy brass andirons and fireguard on the hearth. Fixtures that replicate candlesticks continue the style, and dimmers allow you to reduce light levels when desired. For practicality, augment this moody lighting scheme with discreet recessed fixtures for plenty of ambient light and task lighting where needed.

Consider adding an oversize ottoman. It will do triple duty by serving as a coffee table, an extra seat, and a place to prop one's feet.

Finally, imitate wealthy early colonists by covering your walls with polished wood paneling and your floors with plush Oriental rugs. Both work with the fireplace to warm your room.

American Traditional

Personalize your room by stenciling a favorite quotation around its perimeter. The quote circling this room, *right,* is by Ralph Waldo Emerson.

The furniture styles that originated in colonial times still look right at home from sea to shining sea.

SNUG AND SIMPLY FURNISHED, THE COTTAGES and farmhouses that sheltered generations of rural Americans have left a legacy of comfort as suited to urban high rises and to suburban ranches as it is to log cabins and white-clapboard Colonials.

Beaded-board walls and ceilings evoke porches and kitchens past, setting an informal tone. Paint the beaded board and mantel a

Country European

high-gloss white for a bright but unobtrusive hearth. Keep the millwork simple: A shallow mantel and unfussy columns create an understated background. Add a bright country note with a rim of folkish, hand-painted tiles, such as the classic blue-and-white delft designs.

Furnishings and fabrics with easy-going finishes fit right into country style. A well-worn pine table that started life in a long-ago

Choose colors and patterns to set a mood. Fresh blue and white, *above*, bring sea and sky indoors; red toile, *right*, creates a look of country French.

farm kitchen or a painted secondhand treasure becomes a family-friendly coffee table, its charm enhanced by the scuffs of use.

Treated cotton slipcovers shed spills and can be whisked into the washer when disaster strikes. Country-style interiors are natural showcases for heirlooms and collectibles. Pedigreed quilts and priceless pottery will look right at home, of course, but don't hesitate to incorporate sentimental favorites. Drape a well-worn afghan over a fireside chair or give a child's paint-by-number masterpiece a place of honor on the mantel.

Country European

The appealing mix of comfort, simplicity, and nostalgia that characterizes American country style also marks the traditional interiors of rural Europe and the British Isles. Each region offers a charming variation on the theme. Base your home's decor on the thatched cottages of England's Cotswolds, and you'll lean toward layers of chintz and mantels crowded with china. Take your cues from the South of France or Italy's celebrated Tuscany, and sunshine yellow walls and terra-cotta tiles on the floor will set the mood. *Below,* the clear northern light of Scandinavia illuminates the design scheme. The furnishings have the authentic look of family favorites—handed down, cherished, and given fresh covers in traditional checks and toiles to be enjoyed by a new generation. Painting walls, fireplace, and furniture white is a practical response to Scandinavia's long, dark winters.

The strong squared lines of the Arts & Crafts style are evident in the inglenook, *above.*

Arts&Crafts

AS THE 19TH CENTURY DREW TO A CLOSE, THE GILDED EXCESSES OF THE VICTORIAN era triggered a return to the simple virtues of the past. Whole neighborhoods of snug bungalows with built-in bookcases, benches, and buffets sprang up furnished with the solid, austere oak furniture dubbed Craftsman- or Mission-style. To give your fireside Arts & Crafts appeal, use a color palette featuring cream, terra-cotta, brown, and green. Keep mantel and hearth plain, with square corners and few flourishes. Tile and brick facades with plank wood mantels create the desired geometry.

Simplicity is the watchword of this style: Choose furnishings with no-nonsense lines and sturdy fabrics with subtle patterns. Cover windows with plain, off-white muslin or linen curtains. Impressionistic landscape paintings, matte-finish green pottery, and lamps with copper bases and isinglass shades are ideal accessories. Top wood floors with a flat, woven area rug with stripes or a Native-American-inspired design.

The use of posts and beams to outline the fireplace wall, *left,* is a signature Arts & Crafts detail.

ABOUT THE TIME AMERICA HAD TAMED ITS wilderness, it became nostalgic for it. At the turn of the century, rustic camps and vacation lodges were springing up across the country, from the Adirondacks to Yellowstone Park. The wealthy might forgo big-city comforts to

Laid-BackLodge

rough it without electricity or running water, but the comforting essential heart of every wilderness home was its massive and welcoming stone fireplace.

Today, a fireplace of rugged granite or fieldstone, worn smooth by centuries of weathering, still suggests the snug comfort and relaxed ways of vacation hideaways. Wood-planked ceilings and floors are natural companions to rough-cut fireplace surfaces. Rag rugs and wicker or twig chairs add more natural textures, and a collection of birdhouses or nests brings a touch of the outdoors to the inside.

Though exposed chimneys and open rafters are more familiar elements of lodge-style interiors, the room, *below*, presents a rather genteel variation, surrounding the rough-textured fireplace with conventionally finished walls and wide ceiling molding. The contrast of rough and smooth, light and dark, gives the room a cheerful, contemporary air. The furnishings—brawny fireside chairs of unstripped logs and a tree-slab coffee table—play with the idea of rusticity, exaggerating their woodsy origins. Cushions of mattress ticking soften the chairs' severe profiles, and a needlepoint stars-and-stripes pillow creates a patriotic touch.

Add local color with an old or reproduction map that traces the history of your hometown.

Give a vintage chair, *left,* an unexpected role by using it as an end table.

The rough-hewn furnishings and weathered surfaces of lodge-look rooms trigger vacation memories of camps and cabins.

Smooth Southwest

BOTH LITERALLY AND FIGURATIVELY, THE architecture of the American Southwest has its own vocabulary. Exteriors are fashioned of adobe, a mix of clay, sand, and straw that can be made into blocks or applied like stucco.

The kiva, a distinctive beehive-shape fireplace, echoes the ceremonial chambers of the region's ancient Native American people. Smooth and gently rounded, kivas are built with shallow, angled walls that radiate heat outward more efficiently than many conventional fireplace designs.

You can bring Southwest style to your fireside, even if it's not a kiva. Depending on your tastes, choose a menu of colors anchored by saturated tones of bold teal and coral or sun-bleached shades of terra-cotta and turquoise. Leather-covered sofas and chairs lend an authentic western flavor, especially when they're topped with throws reminiscent of traditional trading blankets. Rustic wood chairs, tables, and cupboards of pine or aspen recall the region's earliest furnishings.

Consider covering your fireplace surround with brightly glazed Mexican tiles or installing an earth-tone floor of oversize matte-finish tiles. Add pottery, baskets, and nubby woven rugs that incorporate some time-honored Native-American symbols such as stylized deer, birds, and fish. True Southwest architecture features heavy structural ceiling beams called vigas. You can add nonfunctional rough-hewn log beams for the same effect.

A kiva-style fireplace in a corner, *left,* plays up the soft curves of the style. Niches in the plaster make simple display perches.

Doing It Your Way

The traditional Southwest style of this living room shows off its friendly nature and is beautifully refreshed with elements of French Country design. The amiable melding of styles from both sides of the Atlantic underscores the similarity of rural design traditions the world around. Because the Southwest-style rough plaster walls and terra-cotta-tiled floors echo the interiors of French country homes, the sunny yellows and true blues of Provence are right at home. Floral and striped fabrics based on traditional European folk patterns cover the throw pillows and sofa cushions. More pillows perch on the broad ledge that forms the base of the kiva-style fireplace. Tiles outlining the arch of the fireplace echo the colors and repetitive motifs of the pillow fabric. Sturdy pine tables and chests, in styles that have been turned out by country craftsmen for centuries, display a collection of pottery pitchers in primary colors. From a niche above the fireplace, a benevolent angel surveys the scene.

Sometimes, fitting a problem fireplace into your design scheme is as easy as painting it into the picture.

20th-Century Eclectic

STORYBOOK HOUSES POPULATED THE NATION'S expanding cities and nascent suburbs in the first decades of the 20th century. Bungalows reflecting a jumble of styles—Spanish Colonial, English Tudor, and French Chateau—boast arched doorways, carved columns, and fireplaces slathered in intricate decorative plaster.

This fireplace, *left*, is typical of the appealing but hard-to-categorize fireplaces in many such homes. If your fireplace seems out of sync with your decorating style, then coax it into compliance. The curving backs on a pair of wicker chairs echo the graceful arch of the fireplace, and a neatly installed modern insert (*see Fireplace Inserts, page 133*) marks an improvement in both efficiency and scale. The asymmetrical, farm-fresh mantel grouping softens the formality of this imposing fireplace.

A monochromatic color scheme can incorporate an out-of-place fireplace and organize a room's diverse design elements. The simple color scheme demonstrates the power of paint to transform a room, creating a natural backdrop for garden-style accessories and fabrics.

Grouping collectibles of similar shapes and colors, such as the ironstone pitchers on the mantel and the mixing bowls on the beaded-board cabinet, gives them more impact.

Brought indoors, weather-worn garden accessories, *left,* such as vintage wheelbarrows and ladders, can function like folk-art sculpture in an eclectic environment.

To create cabinetry in a modern mode, *left,* use pale woods that show little or no graining, and hide or minimize hardware and hinges.

ContemporaryComfort

SLEEK SURFACES AND SIMPLE GEOMETRY FIRST made major inroads into American homes in the 1930s, when Bakelite radios and chrome toasters took their cues from the era's streamlined planes, trains, and automobiles. After World War II, leggy blond Danish Modern furniture and Sputnik lamps ushered in the Space Age.

Contemporary style incorporates a wide range of design influences, from environmental concerns to high-tech processes. Opt for a no-frills look for your fireplace, creating drama with bold angles and unexpected combinations of color or materials. Add screens, tools, and log storage crafted in the same contemporary vein.

Jump start your move to this cosmopolitan look by paring your room down to basics. Bare floors, minimal window treatments, and exposed construction elements such as ceiling trusses or fireplace flues set the stage. Look for clean-lined furnishings that mix modern industrial materials with natural textures such as leather and natural look-alikes such as animal-print fabric.

Choose sofas and chairs with exposed legs rather than skirted styles, then add a splash of glass with a coffee table that reflects its stylish surroundings. In the compact living room, *right,* the fireplace's richly mottled surface is an acid-washed steel plate bolted in place. Slender, hanging halogen fixtures play light across its surprisingly inviting facade.

Above, smooth expanses of pale wood and polished granite visually enlarge the small space. Above the firebox, the granite surround tilts forward to create a shallow mantel. The exposed flue draws the eye upward, to soaring Douglas fir rafters, beams, and trusses. The overmantel, bookshelves, and enclosed cabinets combine solid oak and oak veneer to create an efficient and trim storage wall.

Warm a contemporary room, *right,* with a generous helping of natural light and touch-me textures such as soft leather. An expansive sweep of wood floors promises barefoot comfort.

Look to color and fabric to establish the mood of your favorite fireside.

To find your fireside style, focus on your family's activities, needs, and personality. Whether you're remodeling a family room with a fireplace or building a weekend retreat, you'll keep things simple with uncluttered surfaces and low-maintenance materials.

Establish a country look with wide planks, nailed directly to drywall and left uncaulked to look like barn siding.

Painting the walls, ceiling, and woodwork with the same color will unify a room. Choose a shade of white or off-white to visually expand the room even more.

Tie mismatched seating pieces together by upholstering or slipcovering all of them in the same easy-care fabric. A soft tea-stained floral is a practical, show-no-dirt choice.

If you're adding a fireplace, use the opportunity to build in needed storage for books, games, and collectibles. Combine high shelves for displaying treasures, medium-height shelves for easy access, and closed cabinets that hide clutter.

De-emphasize the formal lines of a fireplace surround with an asymmetrical mantel arrangement of simple objects.

A fireside setting is ideal for displaying collections. The pottery pieces, *below*, get deserved attention on the mantel.

LivingRoom

INCORPORATING A FIREPLACE INTO A DECORATING SCHEME CALLS FOR MAKING ONE very basic decision first: Will you downplay or dramatize your fireplace? If you choose to turn attention away from your fireplace, neutralize it by painting it the same color as the surrounding walls, facing seating pieces away from it, rather than toward it, and leaving the mantel clear of any accessories. But if you, like so many do, consider your fireplace an asset, you can make it the undisputed center of attention.

To emphasize your fireplace, paint walls a contrasting color. The deep green walls, *left,* seem to recede, letting the fireplace take center stage.

Paint your fireplace mantel and surround white and paint walls a deep, saturated color. The effect of the contrast is to make the fireplace say "Look at me!"

Since painting walls in dark shades of green, red, blue, or brown can result in a flat, light-absorbing surface, be sure to use paint with reflective qualities. In most cases, this means selecting an eggshell or semigloss finish. You'll give depth and life to any color

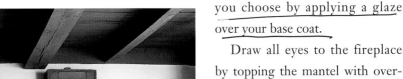

you choose by applying a glaze over your base coat.

Draw all eyes to the fireplace by topping the mantel with oversize artwork. Or draw attention to the firebox with custom-made doors or a hand-wrought screen.

Create an inner circle by grouping chairs, sofas, or loveseats close to the fireplace and defining this intimate gathering spot with an area rug. Be sure to include tables that are within easy reach of all the seating pieces. Leave ample space between the fireplace opening and all furnishings for easy access as well as safety.

A monochromatic furniture grouping allows the fireplace to star. All-alike slipcovers, *left,* confer instant chic on mismatched pieces.

For drama as well as comfort, focus your furniture arrangement around the fireplace.

Fireplaces flourish in user-friendly living spaces such as family rooms and great-rooms. Whether you prefer a slick vent-free see-through, a rugged fieldstone model, or a traditional Williamsburg, fireplaces provide perfect gathering spots for everyday family togetherness—from the bedlam of board game battles to the snuggly quiet of bedtime story reading.

Keep family fireside seating comfortable and casual. Choose relaxed, deep-cushioned chairs and sofas with rounded arms and backs to accommodate sprawling teenagers and the occasional afternoon nap for mom or dad.

Avoid delicate brocades and pale silks. Turn to tough fabrics such as leather, denim, or nubby tweeds. If you prefer light colors, use washable cottons, cotton blends, and man-made fibers with subtle overall patterns that hide dirt. All fabrics should be treated to repel stains and spills.

Add even more comfort with a generous sprinkling of accent pillows and warm and washable afghans, blankets, or throws.

Consider keeping a big basket piled with sturdy, oversize pillows nearby, ready to be pulled out for extra floor seating around a coffee table or up close to a crackling fire. Slipcover the pillows in washable fabric that coordinates with your room's color scheme.

Relegate highly polished coffee tables to more formal rooms. Instead, corral an old trunk or a kitchen table whose legs can be shortened. The distressed surface won't need special care, and table drawers or a trunk interior provide welcome storage for magazines and more.

Keep traffic moving. If family members regularly pass through this space on their way to other rooms, establish a clear path by identifying the fireplace seating zone with an area rug. It's a visual signal that directs foot traffic around the room's cozy core.

See-through fireplaces, *top left,* separate rooms as effectively as walls. Make the most of ample fireside space by backing the sofa with a table and chairs, *top right,* an ideal spot for meals or board games.

Paint dark ceiling beams white, *right,* to brighten and energize a too-dark family room.

Surrounded by cheerful, easy-care furnishings,
a fireplace is a natural magnet for family activities.

Add a dining room fireplace to your menu and
watch family and guests warm up to mealtime.

Look to historical sources to choose appropriate paint colors and accessories for period fireplaces, *left.*

DiningRoom

IT'S HARD TO IMAGINE ANYTHING MORE LIKELY TO CONTRIBUTE TO A RELAXED, gracious meal than a fireplace in the dining room. It conjures visions of friends gathered around the table for long evenings filled with laughter and good conversation warmed by the flickering flames. Depending on the proportions of your room, you can place the table at a right angle to the fireplace or parallel to it. Keep comfort in mind: If you seat diners too close to the fireplace, the heat may be overwhelming. Dress the fireplace mantel with favorite objects and artwork. Paintings depicting pastoral scenes or fruits and flowers are traditional favorites, as are vintage plates. Shine your prized crystal and set out candlesticks and other cherished pieces of polished brass, silver, and copper. They'll gleam even brighter in the glow of a fireplace.

An unadorned mantel, *left,* creates its own drama, as effective at drawing attention as the most elaborate arrangement.

Too many dining rooms lead lonely lives, their fireplaces cold, their charms on display only three or four times a year for major holidays and milestone events. If you'd like to revive your dining room for daily use, then counter its uptight formality with some proven relaxation techniques.

Replace stately mahogany with down-home pine. Put a warm, honey-pine farm table with a timeworn finish under a crystal chandelier, and both will take on a new liveliness.

Place your primly parallel table on a rakish angle instead. Or, set a round dining table on a diagonally placed area rug. Such angles shake up the symmetry of the room, taking the formality factor down a notch or two.

Introduce casual fabrics in tie-on cushions or loose-fitting slipcovers. Swap a demure damask for a bold check, contemporary tea-stained-linen, or exotic ethnic weave. Formal chairs in styles such as Queen Anne often have slip-seats that are easy and inexpensive to recover.

If remodeling is a possibility, consider opening a closed-off dining room to the rest of the house. Freed from its isolation, the

Play down a room's formal architecture by counteracting it with an asymmetrical arrangement of casual furnishings, *above*.

room immediately becomes more accessible and inviting, and the fireplace more visible.

Personalize your dining room. Instead of cookie-cutter decorating, opt for uniquely you colors, furnishings, and accessories. Paint one wall red; mix and match chairs and tableware; or line the mantel with photos from family vacations.

Heavily embossed glazed tiles ensure an eye-catching fireplace, *below*. Keep attention focused there by simplifying other elements, such as window treatments.

See-Through Savvy

See-through fireplaces share their warmth and charm with two rooms. A double-sided masonry fireplace is less expensive than installing two separate fireplaces since the two sides share a common flue and chimney. A direct-vent fireplace unit makes it possible to create a partial wall or peninsula with a double-sided fireplace. This divides an area and defines the different uses. Double-sided fireplaces can be used throughout the house. In 19th-century Victorian homes, grand front halls often had a fireplace that shared a chimney with an adjoining parlor. A common use today is a fireplace that does double-duty by warming both the master bedroom and adjacent master bathroom.

Like Vase w/ivy on table

In the midst of the action or tucked around the corner, a fireplace is a cheerful reminder of kitchens past.

Kitchen

THE KITCHENS OF OLD BOASTED fireplaces big enough to roast a small boar or bake a week's worth of bread. You may not aspire to something quite that ambitious, but if you like the idea of old-fashioned, open-fire cooking and are installing a masonry fireplace, it can be designed to incorporate a grill, a bread oven, and even a crane that will support a kettle for soups and stews.

With or without cooking capabilities, a fireplace gives a kitchen both polish and personality. Site utilitarian fireplaces next to the stove. Others are best enjoyed near the kitchen's eating space and within sight of the

If you prefer bold contrast, plan for additional lighting, since dark surfaces will absorb light. A white mantel, *above*, adds another element of contrast.

work area. A raised hearth brings the fireplace opening up to viewing level for seated diners. Depending on your needs, preferences, and the location of your fireplace, a floor-level opening may be a better option.

For a country European look, consider facing the fireplace with glazed tiles. For a subtle effect, choose natural terra-cotta or match the tiles to your wall color. For more punch, select tiles in exuberant patterns or bright solids.

Fireplace tiles, *left,* flow smoothly into the design scheme when they echo the style and color of the floor tiles, differing only in size.

Once upon a time, every kitchen had a fireplace. In modest country homes—from the thatched cottages of England to the log cabins of America's pioneers—the kitchen was often part of a single large room in which most daily activities took place. Drawing close to the hearth's warmth and brightness, rural families prepared and ate their meals, shared stories, and welcomed friends.

Great-rooms bring us back to this concept of the kitchen as the heart of the home, a gathering spot where a fireplace is essential—and cottage decor is an inspired choice.

Choose natural surfaces and colors for a serene, practical background. Pine floors stand up to hard wear, becoming more mellow with use. Creamy ivory or yellow walls mimic old plaster. *Right*, walls were painted white, then softened and aged with a yellow glaze.

Crank up the charm with an unexpected touch of color. Painting this fireplace surround periwinkle blue, *right*, gives it personality and eye appeal that a more conventional color choice might not have captured.

A cottage-style fireplace craves accessories. Whether you have a passion for teapots, birdhouses, or Blue Willow ware, here's your chance to display it all. Don't be afraid to crowd the mantel with a variety of objects—an artful jumble adds appeal. Add a painting or print with a pastoral theme.

Introduce vintage textiles or new fabrics with an old-fashioned look. Define the fireside sitting area with a rag rug or timeworn Oriental. Faded florals or bright chintz will dress a fireside chair in cottage-style comfort. Slipcovers in fabrics like these can disguise even the most modern seating pieces.

Search tag sales for old table linens such as crocheted tablecloths or pretty linen napkins. If you want to drape a bit of antique fabric along the mantel, be sure to keep it out of reach of random sparks.

Balance your kitchen's high-tech efficiency with a fireside corner filled with cottage charm. You'll be delighted with the results.

There's no need to make a clean sweep when remodeling. *Above,* a pastel mantel is complemented by a ruffled chintz slipcover concealing a worn, but comfortable, chair and balloon valances crafted from old fabric.

Bedroom

Open a small space gracefully with a pair of French doors, *left*. Thanks to the glass doors, this brick fireplace can be enjoyed all day.

IN THE BEDROOM, ALL OF OUR ROMANTIC notions about a fireplace intensify: a fireplace is soothing, inspiring; it draws us out of the everyday and sets us dreaming. A fireplace lends importance to a small bedroom and gives a big bedroom an air of intimacy. The flicker of firelight can calm hard-edged contemporary decor or bestow a glamorous glow on the plainest of furnishings. Whether your style calls for rose-strewn wallpaper and lace-edged sheets or a cool blue-and-white color palette, this private retreat should set a mood that makes you comfortable. Once you've placed your bed to give you the best view of the fireplace, you can begin to fill in the details. If there's room, add a fireside chair or loveseat. A dried flower arrangement suits a bedroom mantel, as does a favorite piece of framed art or a collection of special souvenirs.

Double your pleasure by siting a bedroom fireplace like this practical gas unit, *above*, on a wall that is shared by an adjoining bath.

Make your bedroom fireplace as convenient as possible to use and you're likely to enjoy it more often. While the ritual of bringing in logs, building a perfect fire with kindling, stoking and poking it to keep it burning bright may add to the enjoyment of a blaze in a family room fireplace, a wood-burning fireplace in the bedroom may seem like too much of a good thing. The prospect of storing wood in the bedroom and cleaning ashes out of the firebox leads many homeowners to opt for a gas fireplace instead.

If you haven't looked at gas fireplaces recently, you may be pleasantly surprised to find that once frankly fake logs have been replaced with credible approximations of the real thing. You can choose slender birch look-alikes, Paul Bunyan-size oak imitations, or something in between. For real convenience, consider a gas fireplace with a remote control that will let you turn the unit on and off and control the temperature without ever venturing out of your comfy bed. *(To learn more about selecting a gas-fueled fireplace, including direct-vent and vent-free options, see Natural Gas: Fireplaces and Stoves, page 142.)*

While there is no one right spot for a bedroom fireplace, there are a number of practical and aesthetic considerations that can help you

Although wood fires are romantic, an easy-start gas fireplace may be a better choice for a bedroom.

make the best decision. For example, in an upper-level bedroom, siting a fireplace to correspond with a fireplace in the room below allows them to share the chimney structure, a substantial cost-cutting measure.

If you have a large bedroom, you can create a fireplace wall to serve as a divider. Face the fireplace toward the bed to enclose a cozy sleeping area, and you'll free the rest of the room for use as exercise or home office space. Use a see-through fireplace on the divider wall and you'll double its impact and enjoyment.

In a small bedroom, consider tucking a fireplace into a corner. Southwestern-style fireplaces are often installed this way, and factory-built models specifically designed to fit into corners are also available.

If you have a bedroom where every inch of available wall space is taken up with closets, windows, doors, and indispensable furniture, give the fireplace a room of its own. Anchored by a fireplace, a small sitting room adjacent to the master bedroom can be a haven of privacy in a hectic household. Whether the bedroom and sitting room are open to each other or physically separated, give them a strong visual link by using a common color scheme and similar patterns and fabrics in the two rooms.

A fireplace set in a partial wall, *opposite top left,* allows a bedroom tucked under the eaves to share daylight from a window at the attic's gable end. Recessed ceiling lights, *top right,* keep artwork above the fireplace from getting lost in the shadows. Built-in log storage and seating, *lower left,* expand the impact of a small fireplace. Make a cozy fireside space, *lower right,* more intimate by wrapping the walls with pattern. Use a single color for serenity.

A FIREPLACE WALL IS A SLEEK AND STYLISH WAY TO DIVIDE A LIVING SPACE. Broad or narrow, half-height or ceiling height, the wall creates a shift in purpose, a dividing line for household activities. At the same time, it allows light and air and traffic to flow, maintaining a welcome openness.

Room Divider

When designing a divider, take your cues from the style of the existing room. In this contemporary room, *below*, the fireplace anchors a substantial half-wall that stretches lengthwise to provide privacy for the room on the other side. The geometry of the dividing wall reflects the square openings in the upper part of the room's walls. Careful attention also was paid to the materials used and the scale of all the elements that make up the fireplace wall. The width and height of the

Plan your fireplace wall with space on each side and at the top, *above,* and the room can benefit from borrowed light, an especially important consideration in a home's lower levels.

To make open spaces function for your family, divide and conquer with a fireplace wall.

How romantic are you? In this cozy space, *above,* firelight and candles are the only sources of supplemental light.

fireplace surround match the dimensions of the cabinets that make up the storage wall. Minimal hardware and cabinet fronts as polished and plain as the sleek granite surround create an uninterrupted surface.

Above, the fireplace stands alone in a tall, narrow wall that reaches to the ceiling. It clearly establishes its purpose as a gathering

spot. Rather than shutting out the room beyond, the fireplace wall offers generous views of the surrounding space and shares its light. The choice of a light-color finish for the wall plays down the heaviness of the stone and helps to blend the wall into its surroundings. From any angle the rooms appear seamless and flow together.

It doesn't get cozier than this: The inglenook's built-in benches and woodwork, *above,*

feel like a big hug. Here, a full wall of tile yields a lavish early-1900s feel.

Inglenook

Kivas often have built-in seating, *left,* a practical idea that can be adapted to raised-hearth fireplaces in many other styles.

THE INGLENOOK IS A CHARMINGLY OLD-fashioned idea, and the word itself is equally quaint. Ingle is an ancient British word for a blaze, especially one on a hearth. Tuck that hearth into its own cozy space, flank it with built-in seating and you create the perfect spot for firelight dreaming.

In its purest form, the inglenook is distinctly set off, a sort of room within a room. One way to do this is by building a raised platform so that you step up to the fireplace seating area. Another is to take the opposite approach: Lower the ceiling to differentiate the hearth area from the main portion of the room. Or, build half-walls or bookcases to enclose the inglenook space.

The twin benches of many inglenooks face each other at right angles to the hearth. This arrangement gives the best view of the fire, but space considerations may dictate building seating along the fireplace wall instead. The raised hearths of Southwestern-style fireplaces often incorporate a broad ledge that forms just such a seating spot.

Make your inglenook even more inviting with comfortable seat cushions and plenty of throw pillows. Including wall-mounted lighting or a small reading lamp will encourage fireside reading. Add a small table for drinks and snacks, and bookshelves or a basket to hold books and magazines, and you may find you never want to leave this snug hideaway.

Basement

FOR MANY FAMILIES WITH GROWING PAINS, the search for more living space ends right under their feet. The basement holds precious square footage that, with careful planning, can be made attractive and comfortable living space.

Whether you call the final result a rec room, den, or second family room, adding a fireplace or stove goes a long way to dispel the perception of a lower level room as a dark,

damp, uninviting space. Because there are some special considerations in installing a hearth product into a lower-level space, spend some time researching your options.

Consult a fireplace professional about the best options for basement-level heating. Be ready to tell him or her the size of the space, the number and size of any window openings, and the size and placement of any existing structures.

A fireplace or stove is sure to brighten a basement
remodeling project, but do your homework first.

Wood-burning stoves, *above,* are
an efficient heat source and good
for warming basements and
sending heat to upper levels.

A light filigree metal firescreen,
above right, minimizes the dark
recess of the unlit fireplace in
this bright basement room.

⊏◊⊐ *Decide ahead of time* what you want the fireplace or stove to contribute to the new space. Is it there mainly for aesthetics or do you
want to use it as a heat source? A naturally drafted masonry fireplace
will give you gorgeous flames to look at but may actually draw warm
air from the space. Vent-free appliances are a secondary heat source,
not designed to provide round-the-clock heat.

⊏◊⊐ *Solve any moisture problems first.* While a fireplace or stove does
wick up moisture in a damp basement, the heated air will rise through
the house, depositing moisture on cool surfaces in the upper levels.

⊏◊⊐ *If you have a gas-fired heating system* and your mechanicals are in the
basement, you have a gas line and a flue already in place that may
make a gas-fueled fireplace an easy choice.

⊏◊⊐ *In a cold climate, putting a fireplace on an outside wall* and running a
long chimney up the side of the house may not be the best solution.
The chimney stays cold and may even freeze, especially if the fireplace is not used on a regular basis. This makes it difficult for the
fireplace to heat the air in the chimney, and so it fails to draw properly.

Bath**room**

STEP INTO THAT DEEP TUB, SINK INTO THAT bubble-filled paradise, and soon you're soaking away every major problem and minor ache. Now what could possibly make this sybaritic experience even more soul-soothing? A fireplace, of course.

Because most bathrooms run the gamut from very small to not very big, they lend themselves to dramatic decorating schemes and luxurious small touches. Materials that might be too grand or too expensive to use in a larger space are perfectly suited to a bathroom. You'll get lots of impact from any decorative efforts in this room.

Fireplace Facts

Installing a fireplace in a bathroom requires careful planning and professional expertise. Whether you're remodeling or building, be sure the fireplace is on the agenda as decisions are made about siting the tub, toilet, and sink, and planning for plumbing and drainage pipes. In addition, local building codes spell out a mind-boggling number of dos and don'ts for this small but vital space. Address any restrictions or requirements affecting the fireplace early on.

This sumptuous bathroom, *left,* romances the past with a curvaceous copper tub swathed in canopied splendor and tucked in an alcove created by a bow window. Nearby, a very old marble mantel harbors a very new kind of fireplace: a gas model that can be lit at the touch of a button.

This luxurious contemporary bathroom, *above,* is in an unlikely location—a walk-out basement. A little-used rec room and sauna were transformed into a dream-come-true master bedroom suite. The suite features a three-sided gas fireplace that warms the whirlpool bath area, the larger bathroom space, and the bedroom.

A fireplace can turn the great outdoors into an alfresco extension of your living room.

TOO OFTEN, PORCHES, PATIOS, AND SUNROOMS languish as ho-hum homes to assorted gardening tools and barbeque equipment. Install a fireplace, and instantly you have an open-air living room, ideal for entertaining. Cool nighttime temperatures needn't deter patio dining or evenings of star-gazing. Just gather a little closer to the blazing fire.

Extending the raised hearth, *above,* on either side of this outdoor fireplace helps integrate it with the architecture.

If you have an existing fireplace indoors that's situated along an outside wall, you may be able to install an outdoor fireplace that backs up to it and shares its chimney.

Situate your outdoor fireplace in an area with easy access to the interior spaces where you normally entertain, and guests will naturally find their way there. French doors that open from a living room or dining room to a porch or patio not only add sparkle to the outdoor space, they add panache to the interior as well. Be sure to place a generously sized doormat outside this doorway.

In addition to more substantial furniture, provide your outdoor fireside with plenty of lightweight seating and small tables that can easily be moved closer to or farther from the fire. Don't skimp on cushions and pillows, but be sure they're covered with a fabric that stands up to weather and hard use.

Use low-level lighting that enhances the atmosphere without competing with the fire-light. Candles are a natural choice and are especially effective in large numbers. Cluster them on the mantel and on nearby tables. Outline the perimeter of the patio or the path that leads to it with simple luminaria. Discreet light fixtures in your yard and garden draw the attention of fireside sitters to distant trees and plantings.

Create a cozy feeling at an outdoor fireplace sheltered from the elements, *below*, by dressing the mantel.

Outdoors

Year-round Fun

Enhance the area around the fireplace with plants, flowers, and trees in pots that can be regrouped, changed with the season, or moved indoors when necessary. For a more ambitious project, consider flanking the fireplace with brick or stone planters.

Since your outdoor hearth area is an extension of your home, you may want to keep its decor in harmony with your interior. Or, stepping outside gives you the freedom to choose a new look. Try a tropical color scheme, establish a Tuscan villa ambience, or go Southwestern in your outdoor room.

Time spent around an outdoor fireplace is so pleasant that many people install one even when they live in a climate where summers arrive late and leave early. Extend the quality fireside season by sheltering your hearth in an enclosed porch or a roofed space. Don't hesitate to continue entertaining in this enticing space even when the weather turns cold. Guests will bundle up with enthusiasm for a chili supper served at the fireside or for a cup of hot chocolate and marshmallows toasted over an open fire. An outdoor hearth is sure to become a favorite gathering spot.

Even if you live in northern climes, give your outdoor fireside Southwest style with a sunset palette of glowing golds and rosy pinks, *above*. Shop import stores for affordable furnishings and art objects with south-of-the-border flavor.

close enough to make a cozy conversation area. Set a generous coffee table or ottoman in front of the sofa. An imaginary line drawn from the center of the fireplace should bisect these pieces.

Continue the balancing act with the accessories you choose for the mantel. Framed art work or a mirror can be centered over the mantel, and paired candlesticks, plates, or generous pieces, such as ginger jars, arranged beneath it.

Carried through to the tiniest detail, serene symmetry suits many firesides.

Adding recessed ceiling lights on a dimmer switch, *above,* allows you to augment firelight. Turn the lights down for cozy ambience or up to provide illumination for reading.

Whether you have wall-to-wall carpeting or wood floors, a square or rectangular area rug will anchor the fireside grouping and establish its focal status.

Symmetry by its nature tends to appear formal, even stiff. To relax the look, choose casual fabrics and introduce unexpected colors and textures. Away from the fireplace area, play with the room's equilibrium by adding mini-groupings such as a desk and chair or a single tall secretary or armoire.

IF SYMMETRY SOOTHES, ASYMMETRY ENERGIZES. The eye travels eagerly to take in the varied aspects of a room with mismatched windows, unexpected nooks, or irregular ceiling heights. An off-center fireplace may be more challenging to decorate, but it's also more dynamic.

Asymmetry has its own sense of proportion and balance; it's less obvious than the clear harmony of symmetry. In this family room, *above*, the brawny fireplace with its graceful arched opening meets its match in a broad banquette made possible by extending the hearth around the corner. French doors on the far side of the hearth balance a window placed over the banquette. The proportions of the ample fireside sofa reflect the scale of the built-in seating. A delicate hanging fixture and unexpected elegance of the gold picture frame add a delightful contrast.

If asymmetry appeals to you, you can create the effect in a symmetrical room too. Instead of placing your seating at right angles

To reproduce the sunny rusticity of Italy's Tuscan countryside, bypass boxy fireplaces of brick or stone. Instead, opt for a bold arched style, *above*, with exposed chimney, all swathed in pebbly stucco.

Add pleasing contrast by balancing an off-center furniture placement, *left,* with a symmetrical mantel arrangement.

to the fireplace or to existing walls, give sofas and chairs a quarter turn, creating a livelier sight line.

Arranging furniture on an area rug that's been set on a diagonal to the fireplace makes the process even easier. Sofas and chairs can be placed conventionally to follow the right angles of the rug; the result will be that they have a more visually active relationship with the fireplace.

You can also complement the room's asymmetrical character with your choices for the mantel. If informality is your goal, remember that leaning a mirror or framed piece against the wall rather than hanging it always conveys a more casual approach. *(For more mantel decorating ideas, see page 72.)*

Whether you choose to arrange your furniture symmetrically or asymmetrically in the end, keep the real goal in mind—creating a room that can accommodate solitary reading, quiet talks, or animated conversation, and where guests will feel just as comfortable as family.

Adding a stenciled border or inspirational words draws the eye upward, expanding a small room, *left,* and balancing the visual weight of a large stone fireplace.

In a windowless space, *left,* use glass block to borrow light from an adjacent room while maintaining privacy.

Whether you need to organize an open area or pump volume into a tiny room, start by anchoring the space with a fireplace.

WHILE SPACE IS A LUXURY, AN OPEN FLOOR plan with lots of undefined space often feels cold and unfocused. High ceilings and an absence of walls may leave furnishings adrift.

A fireplace can provide a strong element around which to center furnishings, creating a multipurpose room without conventional walls or doors. Add an ample area rug to further define the area and anchor the grouping.

Unusual Spaces

For a more ambitious solution, simple platforms can be used to create a raised or lowered fireside area, differentiating it from the surrounding space. Adding a low wall defines the perimeter of the space, deftly separating it from traffic flow, but leaving it airily open to the rest of the house.

A case in point is the informal step-down living room, *opposite.* The corner fireplace focuses the space, and its wide, seating-height hearth adds extra value. The mantel extends beyond the fireplace to serve as a display shelf stretching the length of the room and the shelf ties together a series of storage spaces for entertainment and electronic equipment. Finally, books and family photos find a home on three generous shelves.

When building or remodeling a small room that will serve several functions, such as a combination of cooking, dining, and family living, be sure to locate the fireplace on a wall that's visible from every activity area. Creating an angled fireplace wall will increase visibility and add visual interest.

To integrate a fireside area with adjoining spaces, *below,* use the same wall color. Flooring materials and ceiling treatment should flow uninterrupted as well.

A cosmopolitan great-room pares everyday living down to essentials: stylish seating, great views and a fireplace.

Open Rooms

BUY AN EXISTING HOME, AND YOU MAKE THE BEST OF THE FIREPLACE you've inherited. Build an addition or a new home, and you can plan your fireside down to the last detail. Based on all of the not-quite-right spaces you've inhabited, it will be easy to come up with a list of the things you *don't* want; wading through all the possible design solutions will be less daunting given that experience. Here's one possibility, for instance: no formal living room, no separate dining room, no closed-off kitchen. Your answer is an open-to-the-outdoors great-room that can be lived in happily at all hours of the day.

The multi-use space, *left,* is a 36 x 16-foot living room and dining room with a fireplace at its heart. The room is entered from a long gallery that focuses attention on the fireplace wall and the view of the fabulous outdoors beyond.

The see-through fireplace enlivens the entire first floor. It can be enjoyed from the dining area's thickly padded banquette or glimpsed from the adjoining kitchen. Doors on either side of the fireplace open to the broad screen porch with its nearly identical limestone hearth and access to a series of decks. *(For a view from the screen porch, see page 67.)*

Because an all-purpose room gets constant use, it's important to incorporate durable, easy-care materials. Select flooring with a forgiving matte surface, not one that's highly polished and requires constant maintenance. Natural flooring materials such as stone may be initially expensive, but they add value to your home and will never need replacing. Pale, neutral-tone flooring will expand a room and disappear into the background. Dark flooring can compensate for a too-high ceiling, add drama, and make a room seem more intimate.

Traffic Flow

Surrounded by rooms, hallways, and doors, a great-room such as this one, *left,* is more than a gathering spot—it's your home's equivalent of a busy highway interchange.

🡺 Direct traffic with savvy furniture groupings. Create a circle around the hearth, marking the "no through-traffic" space with an area rug.

🡺 Instead of a middle-of-the-room island, fashion an intimate dining space with wall-hugging seating.

🡺 Honor a room's natural pathways between two points. Keep these routes clutter-free, eliminating the need for people to circle around obstacles.

A mantel-free fireplace mounted flush to the wall perfectly accents the minimalist-style room, *left.* Set high in the wall, the fireplace is visible from all points.

FocalPoints

ITS ARCHITECTURAL MASS ALONE MAKES THE fireplace a natural focal point. Add the promise of warmth and comfort, the implications of romance, and the mesmerizing effect of fire, flames—and all that they evoke—and it's hard to believe that anything else in a room could be the center of attention.

Yet, a half-century ago, the ancient hearth encountered a modern electronic rival.

Television sets, growing larger by the decade, vie for attention in rooms where families gather. A walk through almost any neighborhood after dark reveals windows framing scenes of chairs pulled close not to the orange light of dancing flames, but the blue glow of a picture tube.

There's another important candidate for primary focal point: a terrific view. Lucky homeowners who have a view of a snowy mountain range, a lake, a big city skyline, even a pretty tree, will want to see it all and should incorporate the view *and* the fireplace into their plans.

When dealing with competing focal points, here are some approaches to consider:

Group two or more focal points together. Create a niche for the TV on the fireplace wall and a cheery fire can enhance Sunday afternoon football games.

Create multiple focal points. In a long rectangular room with the fireplace centered on an end wall, locate the television set on the opposite wall. In the center of the room, position small-scale sofas back to back, one facing the hearth, the other the TV. Complete the complementary seating areas with comfortable chairs and handy tables.

Build your fireplace on an outside wall. Surround it with windows, and it will draw attention to, rather than compete with, the view.

Think about the room in terms of primary function or most frequent activity. Let that dictate the focus of your seating arrangement. If your family watches TV every night and you light a fire only occasionally on the weekend, downplay the fireplace as a focal point.

Your fireplace can be a team player, cheerfully sharing the spotlight with a big-screen TV or a big-time view.

In the family room topped by a cathedral ceiling, *right,* a circle of stylish, traditional furnishings with a contemporary edge takes in three focal points: an outdoor panorama, a built-in TV, and a broad stone fireplace.

A collection of *sang de boeuf* pottery marches across a fireplace mantel flanked by cabinets, *below*. A lower cabinet hides an undercounter refrigerator.

TVandFireplace

TELEVISION IS A FACT OF LIFE THAT'S NOT always compatible with the stand-alone charm of fireplaces or decorating preferences and needs. In a traditional room filled with delicate brocades or a country setting furnished with down-home pine, space-age black plastic sounds a jarring note.

Tucking the TV behind doors in cabinetry is a neat solution. Whether you want the TV to share the fireplace wall or simply be nearby, be sure the screen is at a comfortable viewing height. A wet bar, bookcases, and enclosed storage can be designed into the same space.

Cabinets need to be adapted with openings at the rear or side to let electrical cords, cables, and other wires pass through. You'll also need to allow adequate space around the set for ventilation, since television sets give off a fair amount of heat.

An easy and inexpensive solution to keeping the focus on the fireplace without giving up the comfort of fireside TV viewing is to house the set on a wheeled, multi-shelf cart that can be moved into the seating area. Roll it out of sight when it's not in use.

Complementing the room's pale walls and carpeting, *below,* white cabinets house a large TV. The unit blends well with the surrounding bookcases.

FengShui

NOTIONS ABOUT WHAT MAKES A HOME LIVABLE DIFFER AROUND THE world. Looking to the serene interiors of the Orient, some Western designers have adopted the principles of feng shui (pronounced *fung shway*), an ancient Asian approach to creating a harmonious environment.

Feng shui is centered on the belief that your home's site, its structure, the objects within it, and the relationship of all of these elements to each other produces either positive or negative energy that affects everything from your health to your financial success.

For example, the belief that unobstructed energy flows in curves similar to those found in nature might suggest choosing a round table for the dining room, flanking a living room entrance with round columns, and rounding, rather than squaring off, the corner of a kitchen counter.

When siting a fireplace, feng shui principles address the dominant, sometimes destructive, nature of fire. A fireplace is never placed in the exact center of a home where its energy might be overwhelming. Water elements—such as a small aquarium or fountain, frequently watered plants, or artwork depicting water—provide balance when placed near the fireplace. A mirror, today's equivalent of ancient gazing ponds, will also balance the hazards of fire.

Feng Shui Basics

Those who incorporate the principles of feng shui in home design believe it creates a positive environment that enhances the lives and fortunes of the home's occupants. Visit your library or bookstore for more information. Some basic terms:

• Chi: The life force that surrounds and infuses all things.

• The ba-gua: This eight-sided diagram enumerates important aspects of life: wealth and power, fame, marriage and commitment, children and the future, helpful people and travel, career, knowledge and family, and health. A feng shui expert can link each of these aspects with various areas within a home, then work to promote positive energy flow.

• Elements: Elements and their colors are fire, red; earth, yellow; metal, white; water, black; and wood, green. Each living space should contain all five elements or the colors that represent them.

The feng shui fireside arrangement, *left,* of chairs and sofa allows a view of the front door. The arrangement also demonstrates how easy it is to blend Eastern ideas with Western belongings to create a comfortable, livable room.

Your fireplace is a fabulous focal point, the ideal setting for dramatic displays of collectibles and color.

ONE OF THE PLEASURES—AND CHALLENGES—OF HAVING A FIREPLACE is decorating the spaces around it. The prospect of producing a pleasing arrangement for this prominent spot in your home may leave you feeling like an artist standing before a blank canvas: eager to begin, and a bit daunted too.

With a mantel you are working with a changeable platform. Any object you put there can be moved or removed, replaced on a whim, changed with the seasons, or left in place for a lifetime.

This is the perfect setting for the things that matter most to you, or just the things that bring a smile. Precious heirlooms qualify for mantel status, as do family photos and quirky finds. If you're a collector, display your treasures, be they bone china, birdhouses, or barometers. Vacation mementos make wonderful fireside companions too. Show off the giant pinecone from the North Woods or the starfish the kids brought home from the shore. If it pleases you to see it every day, this is the place to put it.

Beyond dressing the mantel, your fireplace deserves the full decorative treatment. Consider surrounding it with bold color or bringing out its character with soft yet lush tones.

In summer, or whenever it's not in use, keep your fireplace visually interesting and banish the black hole with bright ideas from a trompe l'oeil screen to a romantic grouping of candles or a painted insert.

decorating a fireplace

Vintage wooden spools once used in textile mills form a grouping of candlesticks that matches the mood of the nearby Shaker-style chair, *left*. Both are perfect accents to the traditional fireplace.

CleanorCluttered

TAKE A LOOK AROUND THE ROOM. IS IT COZILY cluttered or coolly minimal? If your matching loveseats are peeping out from under a dozen chintz-covered throw pillows, chances are you'll lean toward the same feeling of abundance on the mantel. If, on the other hand, your sleek chrome and leather sofa stands in solitary splendor, you'll want to think about choosing a single important object to place above the fireplace.

Bits of the past create a pleasing jumble on a vintage-look mantel, *below,* that was built of new moldings, then antiqued with layers of paint and glaze.

Start by tracing an outline on paper of whatever you plan to hang on the fireplace wall—mirror, framed artwork, sconces. Cut out and tape these shapes to the wall. This allows you to integrate the mantel shelf with the wall display, adjusting the paper shapes as necessary.

Whether you use a few objects or many on your mantel, you'll create the most lively effect by introducing a variety of shapes, heights, and textures. Experiment by gathering a half-dozen decorative items with a range of silhouettes—perhaps a pair of tall, slim candlesticks, some round china plates, a trailing plant in a chunky terra-cotta pot, and a stack of vintage books. Arrange them in varying ways on the mantel, changing their relationship to each other and the amount of space between them. Add or subtract objects until you have a look you like.

Ultimately, any mantelscape that pleases you is successful, but there are some guidelines that may help you to reach that point. When all the items you want to show are the same size, add interest by elevating some of them on decorative boxes or stacks of books. Layer items, with larger ones in the background, smaller ones up front. Give small collectibles impact by grouping them together.

Remember to consider the scale of the room and the fireplace in relationship to the objects on display. A high ceiling may dwarf a delicate arrangement while an oversize painting can overwhelm a small fireplace.

The picture frame above the mantel, *opposite top left,* is actually a weathered window with a series of botanical prints culled from an old book behind each pane. An oh-so-proper symmetrical arrangement of traditional accessories, *top right,* such as a round convex mirror and a pair of Foo dogs, suits this 1826 Boston home. A discarded, rusted sign turns star performer, *lower right.* While its scale is large, the delicacy and openness of the letters keeps it from overwhelming the mantel.

Gather your favorite things for a mantel-top still life that shows off your personal style.

MORE THAN CREATIVE GENIUS ENABLES designers to produce beautiful rooms. Underlying those impressive interiors are some basic design principles that you can use to shape your mantelscape. Among the most important is harmony.

Plan the mantel to contribute to the room's harmony by reflecting the style and colors of the furnishings and fabrics around it.

Is your fireside chair casual, cottage-like, or country-style? Match its mood with country-themed artwork and accessories. Follow the same rule of thumb with any style.

Keep mirror and picture frames appropriate to the overall style of the room. Don't introduce a new color on the mantel. Instead, echo one or more of the primary or secondary colors in the room.

Harmony needn't mean monotony. Vary the shapes, textures, and heights of objects on your mantel for a stylistic composition that's lively too.

Harmonize your fireside wall treatment to work with the room's overall style. The rustic pine paneling, *above,* clearly says country.

BalancingAct

More About Mantels

Here are three approaches to decorating the same mantel, based on principles of balance.

Symmetrical—This even-handed approach to arranging objects is universally popular for a good reason. It creates a restful impression of order and harmony. To achieve this classic look, center a painting or mirror above the fireplace, then flank it with identical objects, such as candlesticks, ginger jars, vases, or statuary. In the top photo, a length of lacy fabric adds a grace note, softening what could be a static arrangement. Note how the vases overlap the edges of the painting, unifying the grouping.

Asymmetrical—A gathering of dissimilar items forms a pleasing arrangement in the center photo. Asymmetry uses careful placement to visually balance elements of different shapes, sizes, and weights. Here, the visual weight of the large framed photo is matched by the combined height of the weather vane and the bulk of the watering can. Asymmetrical arrangements are dynamic, moving the eye and suggesting informality and action.

Radial—In the bottom photo, wall-mounted objects form an arch around the stationary focal point on the mantel. Radial symmetry is based on elements radiating from a central point like spokes fanning out from the hub of a wheel. The plates shown here are not identical, but they are balanced according to size. The two largest plates, with their greater visual weight, logically anchor the grouping at either end.

BrightColor

SOMETIMES WHITE IS just right, but often, it's the default choice, the noncolor we choose when we're too timid to step to the paint counter and say, "Make mine Prussian blue," or "Venetian red please, with a twist of lime." If you've always lived with off-white walls, change may seem scary, but chances are, there's a color out there with your name on it.

When a fireside area has the blahs, a change of color for the walls or the fireplace surround—or both—provides an inexpensive and impressive fix. Ask yourself what character you want the room to have. Neutrals such as brown and gray connote elegance. Straight-ahead primary shades of blue and yellow send out cheerful vibrations. Red signals warmth, passion, celebration.

One good way to choose a room's dominant color is to pick a color in a work of art, area rug, or fabric you plan to use in the room. Contrasting a bold wall color with a white mantel will spotlight the fireplace. The same color paired with a natural wood-stained surround results in a clubby old-world look that integrates the fireplace into the room.

Visit a user-friendly paint store and ask to compare several shades of the color you have in mind. Then be brave. Make that first brushstroke. It's only paint!

It may be that everything you need to know about color you learned in kindergarten, *opposite*. Crayon-bright shades create cheerful spaces.

The red and white elements in the large-scale graphic poster, *below*, repeat the room's bold color scheme, while the French words add a cosmopolitan note.

SubtleColor

When the mood calls for fireside tranquility, surround yourself with soft, soothing shades of your favorite color.

Fabrics, furnishings, and window treatments display an elegant air that marks the room, *above,* as one for quiet contemplation or intimate entertaining. The tiles in the fireplace surround add a delicate color accent.

EVEN SUBTLE COLOR IS A SILENT BUT POWERFUL PRESENCE IN A ROOM, setting the mood as surely as if it came with a sign commanding "Feel happy!" or "Be serene." While saturated colors tend to be energizing, soft shades are almost always restful. If you want to create a fireside haven away from family activities or a retreat to come home to, temper your color choice by mixing plenty of white into whatever paint color you use.

To keep colors upbeat, avoid undertones of gray or blue, opting instead for a base of warm yellow or red. Intensify color impact with a monochromatic scheme that embraces walls, fabrics, and floor coverings.

Pale purple walls surround a fireplace, *below,* that incorporates unexpected materials: The mantel and hearth are made of concrete. This subtle background is the perfect backdrop for the richly colored surround.

If you're not sure you're ready to commit to painting your walls, you can test a color's impact on the room with several yards of inexpensive fabric in the color family you're considering. Wrap a chair, drape a length over the back of a sofa, hang a panel at the window to allow daylight filtering through the fabric to color the walls. Live with the color for a day or two, noting how it changes in natural and artificial light and gauging its effect on your mood.

Remember that paint colors can look very different depending on the finish. A high-gloss finish intensifies the color, but also shows every irregularity on a wall surface. Flat paint minimizes surface flaws, but absorbs light, dulling the color. For most rooms, an eggshell or semigloss finish is just right.

Keep an unlit fireplace from being dark and dreary; use a little creativity to make it bright and appealing.

OutofSeason

THOUGH THERE ARE FEW SIGHTS MORE WELCOMING THAN A BRIGHTLY burning fire, the black hole of an unlit fireplace can be a dismal eyesore. In the 18th century, fastidious fireplace owners covered openings with close-fitting boards painted with flowers or still lifes designed to look attractive while keeping out drafts, soot, and small animals. Victorians favored fireboards that were decoupaged, covered with wallpaper, or made of papier-mâché. By the 1920s, central heating had made fireplaces redundant, but so strong was their nostalgic appeal that new homes often included purely decorative fireplaces with electrical outlets that gave homeowners the option of plugging in ersatz logs.

If you've inherited one of those strictly-for-looks fireplaces or are looking for a summertime fill-in, options range from a simple massing of dried flowers to a whimsical trompe l'oeil screen.

Wide fence pickets, *left,* are painted with stripes and hinged in accordion-fold fashion to create a fanciful fireplace screen. A hearth refurbished with marble cladding, *above,* maintains its focal-point status in warm weather with a luscious floral arrangement.

Look to these solutions to add a stylish glow to an unlit fireplace:

☞ *Create the impression* that a fire is just moments away from being lit by stacking a generous number of logs on the grate. Birch logs are an excellent choice. Their papery texture lends interest while their white bark brightens the space.

☞ *If the fireplace receives* a fair amount of daylight, fill the opening with greenery. A single large brass urn with glossy philodendron leaves spilling over its sides is a graceful complement to a traditional room. Geraniums or other cheerful summer annuals in an oversize straw basket—natural or painted white—would suit a country-style great-room.

☞ *Follow the lead* of American colonists who opted for freestanding figural fireboards, often solemn-faced servants or winsome children. Check library books to find a period portrait, make a copy, enlarge it, and trace it on to plywood. Use a jigsaw to cut out the shape, then paint in the details. Set the figure into

This bedroom fireboard, *below,* was cut to fit the arched opening of the firebox. A grouping of over-scaled porcelain pieces, as delicate as the room's pastel color scheme, was painted against a charcoal gray background that simulates the darkened fireplace opening.

Faux Firelight

You can romance a dark firebox with a dreamy display of chunky candles. Look for wrought iron, pewter, and other metal candle racks or "trees" in mail-order catalogs and candle shops. These multi-armed stands hold 6 to 12 pillar candles in staggered rows. You can also create your own display without a ready-made candleholder. Avoid placing the candles directly on the hearth. Instead, rest each on a heatproof base of metal or glass to catch the drippings. To vary the height, prop the candle with its accompanying dish on a clay flowerpot that's been turned upside down.

Glowing Bright and Safe

Follow these tips to keep your glowing display of candles safe:

- Limit the number of candles. Open the flue if your fireplace is operable, and leave the glass doors open.
- Otherwise, move the candles toward the front of the firebox.
- Put a decorative metal screen or tall andirons in front of the candles.
- Be sure the room is adequately ventilated; candles require a surprisingly large amount of oxygen.
- Keep a fire extinguisher on hand.
- Never leave burning candles unattended.

Candles light a fireplace in this peach-toned Southwestern-style room, *above.* Tall andirons are a good choice for an extra-tall fireplace opening.

notched wooden blocks or brace the back to allow it to stand. Not a people person? Outline an oversize basket or vase of flowers instead, and paint the posies to match the colors in your room. Easiest of all: Cut plywood to fit the firebox, paint it, then stencil on a simple pattern.

Objects that are weathered or occur naturally outdoors enliven an unlit fireplace. Heap an oversize platter with a trove of shells and bits of driftwood anchored in a base of pale beach sand. Pile a shallow tray high with an assortment of spiky pine cones. Shop flea markets for vintage painted shutters to prop in front of the fireplace.

MANTELS ARE MADE FOR CHRISTMAS. THEY'RE the spot to hang your stockings, of course. But don't stop there. Combine nature's bounty with as much glitter and ribbon as suits you to produce a display you won't want to take down in January.

Work with the elements already in place. In the living room, *above*, an ornate tin-framed mirror and blue-and-white ginger jars remain in their year-round spots to anchor a lush arrangement of flowers, berries, and greenery.

The juxtaposed textures combine for a dramatic effect. Smooth, red tulips are tucked among gracefully drooping sprays of cedar and punctuated by spiky branches of crimson berries. To incorporate fresh flowers into your holiday mantel display, use slim plastic tubes—available from a florist—to hold individual flower stems in water.

While plenty of flowers and greenery are available at retail outlets, don't ignore the bounty in your own backyard. The perfect

HolidayTime

Coordinate colors: The red herringbone-pattern brick in the fireplace interior, *above,* plays up the red in holiday decorations.

snip of evergreen or berry-laden branch may be just outside your door.

Let your fireplace style dictate the direction your holiday decorating takes. The free-form swag, *below*, mimics the curves of the Southwestern fireplace. For a long-lasting, low-maintenance arrangement, choose plant materials that don't need to be watered. Myrtle, safflower, and millet berries maintain their shape and color as they dry. Keep the decorations clear of the fireplace opening and remove arrangement before it's dry to the point of being brittle.

While the mantel stars in your holiday decorating, don't isolate it. Repeat the materials, colors, or themes used on the mantel in nearby areas to unite the room visually.

Add a little local color. Native greenery, *below*, and locally grown wildflowers and berries in this swag connect the indoor scene to the desert outside.

Mantels in simple, traditional American styles can shine in holiday decking that goes beyond an abundance of the expected evergreens. Stretch your imagination by using something other than the familiar color choices and materials. Applied with a light hand, you'll create a unique, dramatic setting.

 Shift the color selection from bright reds and greens to subtle hues. Or, eliminate one hue altogether; traditional Christmas red is absent in the room, *below*. Instead, a sage-like shade of evergreen in the eucalyptus swag—which dips, curves, and trails off the mantel—contrasts with the all-white background.

Extend the life of fresh greens by misting them daily with a spray bottle.

 Use period materials, arranged in the traditional form. The antique paneled fireplace surround in the New England home, *right*,

shows how to use materials from garden and pantry to create Early American-inspired embellishments. Create a similar look by using pineapples—the colonial symbol of hospitality—dried apple sections, cranberries, and pinecones. The muted tones of these plants work well with the rich golden color on the walls and ceiling.

 Start gathering early. Natural materials can be collected and dried year-round to create yuletime wreaths, swags, and topiaries. Look for pods, seeds, cones, and berries.

Wiring together generous amounts of greens creates a swag that needs no embellishment, *below*. Decorating a holiday mantel in a fashion that honors the style of your home and fireplace, *right*, can be a satisfying way of connecting to Christmases past.

You can bring out the best in your fireplace with an imaginative quick fix or a full-blown remake.

hearth
renovation

A CLASSIC FIREPLACE STYLE CAN LOOK TIRED OR just appear out of sync with the rest of the room. Changes made earlier may not have helped. A poorly done remodeling can strip even the most elegant fireplace of its charm.

Then comes the question of how much remodeling to do—major surgery or just a bit of sprucing up? Simple cosmetic changes include painting the fireplace mantel and surround or replacing them with a different style or an update of the same style. A facade of colorful tiles neatly updates a sad brick surround. There's no need to remove the brick. Just mount the tiles directly on the brick surface with mortar. Feeling more ambitious? Incorporate a modest fireplace in a wall of bookcases or built-in seating to create an important focal point.

When you're ready to rejuvenate your fireplace, you'll find inspiration in these stories of fireplaces with a new spark.

In the playroom, *left,* jazzy black and white tiles in two sizes cover boring brick with bold graphics to establish a playful mood.

Before&AfterTales

A FIREPLACE THAT'S JUST ALL RIGHT MAY NOT be just right for you. The self-admitted persnickety homeowners of this fireplace, *below*, brought their old fireplace up to snuff in two steps: They replaced the existing mantel with one milled to match cabinetry in other parts of the house. Then they refaced the multicolor marble surround, hearth, and manteltop with a lush, mauve-hued granite similar to the stone used in the kitchen and dining room.

If your fireplace mantel tone is out of tune with its surroundings, a simple change in paint color that integrates it into the overall color scheme is a quick way to bring it into harmony with the rest of the house.

To take that harmony up a notch, choose an existing trim in your home with a profile you like, and have new fireplace molding milled to match. This isn't necessarily an expensive proposition. The high-volume mills that make the woodwork trim found at home centers and lumberyards can use the same machinery to produce any custom shape by creating a cutting knife that will produce the

new pattern. Also, check the prefabricated mantels for an acceptable substitute.

To save a bit of money on custom-milling, keep in mind that you don't need pricey woods like cherry, walnut, or maple if you intend to paint the mantel. Instead, request paint-grade lumber.

Sometimes, a totally new look is required. Cinderella transformed for the ball had nothing on this fireplace, *right*. It started life with what the homeowner called "nondescript, noninteresting brick and a wimpy mantel."

Hanging an extra-long, rectangular mirror above a mantel, *right,* can emphasize the fireplace's width, creating sleek horizontal lines. Reflecting an arrangement of favorite objects doubles the impact. This custom-made mirror's length required the framer to combine two picture frames.

Before

When you're looking for an affordable shortcut to elegance, do as these homeowners did: Opt for a fireplace surround kit. Research existing styles in manufacturers' catalogs or view the finished models on display at local fireplace shops. For a truly professional look, create a custom panel above or on each side of the fireplace, incorporating matching molding available from the fireplace kit's manufacturer. Painting the entire surround the same color as the woodwork in the rest of the house will keep your freshly refurbished fireplace from looking like an afterthought.

The subtle grain and color changes in marble, slate, limestone, and other natural materials make it especially important to look at samples in the setting where the material will be used. Consider undertones of pink, yellow, brown, or gray when selecting complementary paint for nearby surfaces.

Large scale tiles—like these 12-inch cream and taupe marble squares—create an appearance similar to a single slab. Smaller tiles, set in grout, form a more informal grid. Marble can be polished, or *honed*, a term that denotes a matte, rather than a glossy, finish.

When the heftier proportions and more formal lines of a new fireplace, *above,* made the ceiling molding look out of place, new, wider cove molding added balance.

Before

Stuck with a hopelessly inappropriate
fireplace? Take heart—even a rough-hewn
misfit can be tamed by clever design.

SticksandStones

Integrating a rough stone fireplace into a traditionally styled room is a tough assignment. An asset in a rustic lodge-look home can seem like an obstacle in a more refined space. But the owners of this Seattle home found a clever way to bring out the beauty of their diamond in the rough.

They designed and built an impressive wall of glass-fronted cherry cabinets that embrace the fireplace in a handsome frame.

To recess your fireplace and minimize its bulk, plan for cabinetry on each side that is deeper than the fireplace, stepping out and away from the wall. A generous mantel can act as a bridge between the cabinets. When the fireplace is a heat-circulating model that requires venting, the mantel can be designed to conceal the vents that distribute warm air.

Wrap the tops of the cabinets and fireplace with molding to tie them together.

Rather than trying to overpower the rough-hewn character of the stone with an elaborate design, keep the cabinets' outlines simple. Curving lines and ornate hardware will clash with and underscore the fireplace's rusticity, but flat, recessed-panel doors, strong vertical lines, and understated hardware complement its strength.

A bonus of any makeover can be added display area and storage. Include glass shelves to show off collectibles and enclosed lower cabinets to house stereo equipment and provide space for videos, CDs, and other miscellany.

Carefully placed lighting dispels a rustic fireplace's sometimes gloomy appearance, playing up the liveliness of the stone. Mount several recessed fixtures in the soffit to wash the stone with light, highlighting its texture and bringing out subtle color variations. Here, an added spotlight focused on the mantel draws attention to the owners' hand-built "pond yacht," a buoyant symbol of the room's makeover.

The hulking and soot-stained stone fireplace, *left,* sat in this living room like an 800-pound gorilla, definitely impossible to ignore. Now cleaned up, well-lit, and flanked by cleverly designed cabinetry, it's a strong and handsome element in a wall worthy of attention.

SpaceProgram

CHANGING THE FUEL SOURCE OF A FIREPLACE can create new concerns. For this homeowner, replacing a shallow, coal-burning fireplace with an up-to-date natural gas unit posed a special problem in remodeling a 1908 San Francisco home. Plans to convert a former dining room into an expansive great-room off the kitchen called for an ambitious makeover that included a fireplace wall incorporating bookcases, storage, and seating.

The project architect determined that the fireplace, on an inside wall of the home's second floor, needed a new flue, one that would have to go up through the third-floor fireplace's chimney. Because the fireplace opening in the dining room was unusually small, a zero-clearance, prefabricated model was chosen. Still, the space was too tight. The solution required bumping the fireplace out into the room to create enough space to accommodate the flue. Happily, this created a nook on each side, cozy corners for the planned bookcases and bench.

When a fireplace remodeling plan demands extra inches, consider the space in surrounding rooms. If the fireplace wall backs onto a room that's large enough to give up a

Before

little space, you can recess built-ins on either side of a new fireplace more deeply, thanks to the borrowed square footage.

While open bookshelves are attractive, remember to include closed storage space to stow board games and other clutter. Fireside cabinets can attractively conceal current entertainment and media electronics or be prewired for future equipment. A hinged bench seat provides more storage.

Many modern fireplace units make it possible to retrofit nearly any size space. A natural gas colonial-look fireplace, *right,* replaces a tiny green-tiled Mission-style coal unit.

Memories of the sunny climes of southern France
inspired the transformation of a 1970s fireplace.

WHEN YOU'VE DECIDED THAT REFURBISHING THE FIREPLACE REQUIRES more than a cover-up, you're free to create an entirely fresh look. Believe it or not, the fireplace pictured here was once encased in a 1970s-style, floor-to-ceiling, white fiberglass surround. The homeowners had honeymooned in the idyllic French countryside of Provence, so they chose the sun-drenched old-world style of that region to replace the room's dated decor.

When the old fiberglass material was removed, a new wall was created with wood framing, plywood, and layered drywall. A finish of drywall mud simulated the look of vintage plaster. To contrast with the vibrant yellow of the walls, the exposed chimney was left unpainted.

FrenchTwist

To remake your fireplace in the country-European style, look to blue and white tiles, a key element in establishing an old-world mood. Beginning in the 1600s, the Dutch dominated glazed tile production, and their universally appealing delft tiles decorated fireplaces in village cottages and grand homes throughout Continental Europe and Great Britain. You'll find new tiles in similar patterns widely available. Consider buying enough tiles to use as a backsplash or accent tile in a kitchen or bathroom, visually tying the new fireplace to the rest of the house.

You can mix fabrics freely by sticking to simple patterns and a consistent color scheme.

Mail-order catalogs are a good source for accessories with South-of-France charm. In the family room, *left,* a copper flower holder and chunky glazed pottery candlesticks in bright colors with fruit and flower patterns draw attention to the painted wood mantel.

More Than a Pretty Face

Sure your fireplace looks great. You love the romantic aura and the whole home and hearth thing. But while traditional wood-burning fireplaces warm our hearts, many are also notorious heat thieves, sending an astonishing 90 percent of their warm air up the chimney and feeding only 10 percent into the room. You can make an open-hearth fireplace more heat efficient by refitting the fireplace with a prebuilt, recirculating insert with glass doors. These convective fireplaces use a series of vents to draw in cold air, heat it, then send it back out into the room. Vents can be placed inconspicuously so that the aesthetics of your fireplace are minimally affected. Prebuilt fireplace inserts are essentially wood-burning stoves that will use your existing fireplace opening and chimney to give you a reliable heat source.

TudorRescue

THOUGH FIREPLACES ARE A MUCH-DESIRED AMENITY, few houses are sold by hearth alone. If the location is right, remember that the fireplace can be redone. A picturesque 1932 Tudor-style cottage had an abominable paneling fireplace surround. The homebuyers were undeterred. Given the opportunity to create an old-world-style fireplace in keeping with the spirit of the house, they did some homework. The result is a limestone structure with a gently curved arch capped by a distinctive keystone.

When planning an ambitious remake, research is key. Once you've settled on a style and materials, sketch your final design out in detail, on paper or with the help of a computer program. One way to "test" a design is to make a full-size cardboard model; put it in place to see how your dream fireplace fits in the room—and it's much cheaper to revise a design in cardboard than in stone. Take your ideas to a professional designer or architect. Have more than one mason bid the job, and ask to see the mason's existing work. You're looking for a skilled craftsman who takes pride in attention to detail.

Before

While it looks massive, the limestone fireplace, *right,* is only 5 feet high and 6 feet wide, in keeping with the home's compact size. The mason retained much of the original fireplace structure, *below,* removing only the decorative brick surrounding the firebox.

Vision and craftsmanship turned a hopelessly
remuddled fireplace into a limestone beauty.

NEW-CONSTRUCTION CONDOMINIUMS ARE NOTORIOUS FOR THEIR BLANDNESS, and this two-story unit was no exception. Apart from bump-out windows that offered breathtaking views of Vancouver's English Bay, the rooms were feature-less white boxes. The owners opted for a full-scale revamping of the space, including a redesign of the run-of-the-mill fireplace.

CondoConcrete

When you take on a condo remodeling, you may find you have problems not faced by most homeowners. Local ordinances and building covenants may restrict major structural changes. In this project, the room layout remained unchanged, but rooms were gutted to create a new personality. The result is a striking new fireside that successfully combines three strong focal points: the fireplace, the view, and the artwork.

One way to accomplish this in a shared-space home is through careful attention to balance to keep one element from dominating. Got a spectacular view? Don't settle for a mild-mannered fireplace and undistinguished art. Do cut down on visual clutter by minimizing color and pattern to allow multiple focal points to flow gracefully together, rather than compete.

Here, a sandblasted concrete fireplace surround that juts out beyond the wall forms a base for a single large-scale piece of art. With no frame around the art, an absence of window coverings, and a pristine mantel, the viewer's gaze moves fluidly—with delight— around the room.

Suspending several halogen spot-lights from a high ceiling, *opposite,* lets light play across the mantel and artwork and calls attention to the surface of the fireplace wall.

SimplyCountry

SOMETIMES, THE SALVATION IS AS SIMPLE AS paint. This fireplace seemed like the punchline to a bad joke: What's black and white and ugly all over? White stones seemed to float in black mortar, like marshmallows in chocolate pudding.

The "mortar" had been painted black to match the dark stain on the mantel and ceiling beams. The new homeowners had a better idea: Keep the mantel's natural wood look, but paint the fireplace face, the walls, and the exposed timber trusses white. The lighter surfaces reflect, rather than absorb, light, illuminating the vaulted ceiling, giving the dining room a lift, and visually expanding its dimensions.

By removing the walls and ceiling around a fireplace and letting the exposed chimney stretch to the rooftop, you can anchor an otherwise featureless space. This dining room was originally the modern ranch home's living room; a previous remodeling had rearranged the interior spaces. The house is only decades old, but the room takes its decorating cues from the centuries-old traditions of the surrounding farm country.

Establish an inviting country feel with long-wearing pine planking in a warm honey color. Expand the room visually by wrapping the flooring around the fireplace, allowing it to flow seamlessly into adjoining rooms.

Before

Choosing antique and vintage-look furnishings with spare lines and sculptural simplicity is a sophisticated approach to country decorating. Extend the look to the hearth with handsome hand-wrought iron tools. A hefty, rough-hewn mantel can be the perfect foil for a large-scale, simply-framed work of art.

In this room, the artwork's frame extends just beyond the broad beam that crosses the fireplace wall, carrying the eye upward. A pair of slim metal urns on curving legs adds a modern note while fulfilling a practical function—disguising an air vent on the fireplace wall.

Stripping a ranch home to its structural bones can open it up to a contemporary-country look, *right*. Warm wood tones play beautifully against a stark white background.

In a high-style dining room with clutter-free country charm, the power of paint transforms an ugly-duckling fireplace.

AN ANTIQUE MANTELPIECE IS AN ASTONISHINGLY VERSATILE BIT OF architectural furniture. It can slip seamlessly into a period room or jolt a contemporary room to life by adding a note of surprise.

Vintage mantels don't come in standard sizes; if you're planning to pair a new fireplace with an old mantel, always choose the mantel before installing the firebox. When you're looking for an antique mantel for an existing fire-

VintageChoices

place, take along careful measurements of the firebox and the width and height of the fireplace wall. You can't vary much, but adjusting the width of the stone or tile around the fire-box can help accommodate a vintage mantel that's not quite the right size.

In general, you'll want to keep the fireplace's overall dimensions in scale with the room's size and height. You can achieve a daringly stylish look by using a fireplace that is dramatically oversized or deliberately diminutive, but be sure it conveys a decorative choice, not an aesthetic blunder.

Carry your fireplace's measurements with you so you can buy with confidence. The heavily carved mantel, *right,* was found in Mexico.

Retrofitting Reminders

There's more than aesthetics involved in retrofitting a fireplace. Be sure to have an expert assess the condition of your chimney and hearth.

◁▷ One of the most desirable properties of a fireplace is good draw. If your existing fireplace has this ability to maintain a fire by efficiently moving warm and cold air through the chimney, be wary of structural alterations that change the relationship between the size of the flue opening, the smoke chamber, and the firebox. If it doesn't draw well, now is the time to make things right.

◁▷ Local building codes spell out rules for installing a new fireplace or renovating an existing one. Even if all you're doing is replacing your mantel, it's important to be aware of safety issues covered in these codes, such as the width of solid masonry required between the firebox and any nonmasonry material, such as a wooden mantel.

◁▷ Changes that involve the firebox require even more vigilance. A reputable professional installer will follow local codes governing the required gap between the firebox and floor joists or framing.

There's a great deal of satisfaction in tracking down and fitting a piece of the past into your fireside scene.

Advances in styling and technology make building a fireplace into an add-on space or home remodeling project easier than ever.

No fireplace? No problem! Remodeling an existing room or adding more space to your home presents the perfect opportunity to plan that dream fireplace you've always wanted. Before you lose yourself in romantic visions of blissful evenings spent before a crackling fire, stop for a reality check. Better yet, sit down with pen and paper, and make an actual checklist. Here are some questions to consider:

What types of fireplaces fit your budget? While a wood-burning masonry fireplace built on-site gives you the widest range of design possibilities and produces a flickering, fragrant fire that satisfies the senses, it's also the most expensive option.

What do you want from a fireplace? Listing such factors as size, appearance, ease of operation, efficiency, and heat output in order of importance to you will help you narrow the range of product you'll want to consider for your building project.

Do local building or environmental codes governing fireplaces dictate the range of fireplace types you can consider? In some parts of the country, concerns about air quality put limits on wood-burning fires. In other areas, vent-free fireplaces may face restrictions.

Are there structural limitations or requirements you need to factor in? A masonry fireplace may need additional structural support. Or the spot you've chosen for your fireplace may preclude using conventional venting or make it difficult to run a gas line in. Consult with a hearth-product professional early in your planning process, and you'll avoid the disappointment of setting your heart on a fireplace type that just isn't right for you.

adding
a fireplace

Remodeling a small room? Why not warm it with a fireplace, then make it a larger-than-life dream haven, *left,* with a soaring ceiling and glass walls?

Right-OnRemodel

BEFORE YOU START TO ZERO IN ON FIREPLACE types and styles, take some time to assess the strengths and weaknesses of the space you plan to remodel. Ask yourself how your family uses the space, how the traffic pattern could be improved, and whether constant clutter means that building in more storage space should be a priority. Are you satisfied with the amount of natural light in the room? Does the room feel uncomfortably isolated from the rest of the house? The answers may open up some surprising design possibilities.

Replacing an interior wall with a fireplace in a partial wall can be a clever way to deal with a number of common drawbacks. By installing a fireplace on an inside wall, you'll free exterior wall space for additional windows. Rooms open up to each other, sharing the light that flows over and around the new partial wall. And a double-sided fireplace that serves both rooms adds even more value.

You'll expand the visual impact of an open floor plan by painting adjoining rooms, *above and right,* in the same colors.

A dividing wall is a natural spot for built-in storage, from open shelves to custom-designed niches for electronic equipment. The bright and airy spaces, *left and below,* owe much of their charm and workability to the openness of the floor plan. The fireplace placement is a key element in creating an organized floor plan. Partial walls mark a change in function or focus, defining space while still allowing rooms to flow together.

In this remodeling, the original full wall that separated the dining room and living room was replaced with a three-quarter-height wall that houses a two-way, direct-vent gas fireplace. The fireplace vents to the side, exchanging air intake and exhaust directly through the exterior wall, thus requiring no vertical flue or chimney.

Space-dividing, direct-vent gas fireplaces are also available in versions that offer glass on three or four sides, making sleek peninsula or island designs possible. What you'll see on the exterior wall is an opening that looks a bit like your clothes dryer's exhaust vent.

Before

A see-through fireplace, *left,* was a key element in transforming this home from dark to light, airy, and stylish.

Addition Options

WHILE YOU'LL SAVE MONEY if the exterior footprint of your addition is a square or rectangle with no jogs or bumpouts, don't settle for an unimaginative box that's just tacked on to provide more square footage. Make your fireplace the centerpiece of a room where creative interior details make the difference.

Add visual interest with an unusually shaped hearth or an eye-catching oversized

Think outside the box to find clever solutions like these: A bowed roof, *above,* keeps upstairs views unobstructed and is substantial enough to visually carry the brick chimney.

mantel. Balance a big fireplace with generous windows that take advantage of an appealing site. Locate the fireplace on the wall opposite the room's entrance to emphasize its importance as a focal point.

Window seats and storage and entertainment units, *left,* create an interior architecture that relieves the monotony of square corners and uninterrupted walls.

Use soffits and dropped ceilings to create subtle separation for areas devoted to a specific function, such as dining or listening to music.

Consider building the addition a step or two down from the adjoining room. This lends the room a sense of drama, a feeling that you're entering a special place.

Link the new room to the rest of the house by carrying at least one major element—flooring, paint color, or fabric—from one of the adjoining rooms.

Facing Up to It

Choosing a fireplace facing is strictly a matter of personal taste. For informal floor-to-ceiling fireplaces, stone veneer or rock set in mortar are common choices. Stucco will give a more elegant, old-world look. With a conventional wood mantel, you'll be choosing a material to fill the space—called the gap, or slip—between the mantel and the firebox. Here your choices include new or antique tile, brick, or quarried materials such as slate, marble, or limestone. Stone or marble mantels were originally made to fit the fireplace opening with no need for intervening material, but if you're retrofitting an antique mantel and need to fill a gap, a marble tile in a complementary neutral shade is a good choice.

What's Involved

WHETHER YOU'RE ADDING A NEW FIREPLACE OR REFITTING AN EXISTING ONE, you'll make the best decisions by first boning up on the basics of styles, installation methods, and approximate costs. Consult a variety of professional sources, from architects and contractors to fireplace shops and hearth-product trade associations. (*Start with Resources, page 158.*)

Relatively lightweight and easy to install, a direct-vent gas fireplace, *below,* is a good choice for a second-level bedroom, sitting room, or office.

⊏▷ *Wood-burning fireplaces*: Most new fireplaces are prefabricated units that fit in a relatively small space and are straightforward to install (*see opposite page*). Similarly, you can upgrade an existing fireplace without giving up the sound and smell of a natural wood fire by installing a fireplace insert. These insulated metal fireboxes circulate air to increase heating efficiency by as much as 75 percent. When adding a new, built-on-site masonry fireplace, remember that the concrete, bricks, and masonry of conventional fireplaces require additional structural support.

⊏▷ *Gas-fueled fireplaces*: Gas fireplaces require little structural alteration. They can be vented through a conventional chimney or directly through an exterior wall. If you're retrofitting a wood-burning fireplace with a gas appliance, you'll need to have the existing chimney relined with aluminum or stainless steel, since gas fires can reach very high temperatures. Where natural gas is not available, propane may be an option. Ventless fireplaces are convenient for interior walls but are not approved for use in all municipalities.

⊏▷ *Stoves:* Today's cast-iron and steel stoves are a cost-conscious, fuel-efficient heat source. You'll find models that burn wood, coal, gas, or wood pellets. (*For more information, see Fireplace Options, page 130.*)

Guarantee a successful fireplace installation by choosing the
right hearth product for you and relying on professional help.

The Simple Steps to Success

Corner fireplaces need little floor or wall space, fitting
smoothly into small rooms or rooms where wall space
is broken up by multiple windows and doors. Here, a
gas fireplace with direct-vent technology uses a short
section of pipe on an exterior wall to send exhaust
fumes out and take fresh air in. Because this hearth
product draws in air from the outside, rather than the
room, it's a more efficient heater than a conventional
wood-burning masonry fireplace. After a gas line is
installed and electrical circuits provided for the fireplace blower, the unit is framed in place. In the final
step, drywall is put over the framing lumber and
painted. Plan on about a week to complete this type
of installation.

& ot

Explore the intriguing alternatives to a traditional hearth, from wood-burning stoves to do-it-yourself faux fireplaces.

BEYOND THE CONVENTIONAL FIREPLACE LIES A WORLD OF ALTERNATIVES. When you want the cozy hearth experience but a fireplace isn't right for you, look to the impressive array of stoves, freestanding outdoor appliances, electric virtual fireplaces, and just plain fakes.

For many of us, the word *stove* conjures up the Hollywood Western variety—a soot-belching, pot-bellied behemoth, surrounded by a circle of crusty old codgers gathered in the general store.

In contrast, today's sleek steel and cast-iron stoves are high-tech wonders. Worries about depleting forests have resulted in fuel-efficient wood stoves that produce more heat with less wood. Air-quality concerns have led to clean-burning stoves with low emissions levels. And unlike the only-black days of yore, you can have a stove in shades that range from forest green and creamy ivory to candy-apple red.

A stove is a smart choice when your concerns go beyond romantic atmosphere to a product that will be a reliable source of heat in general and a reassuring backup for weather-related and other emergencies when normal heating and cooking appliances may not function.

A visit to your local hearth-products store or home center will reveal other fireside options. For indoor use, consider one of the electric heaters with convincing-looking logs—some with appropriate crackling sound effects. Outdoors, freestanding deck and patio fire appliances bring the fun of vacation-time campfires close to home.

A stove can add an authentic note to a period-style room. The serene Victorian Gothic parlor, *left,* features a cream-color stove that fits easily into the pale color scheme.

WoodStoves

LIKE A FIREPLACE, A STOVE NOT ONLY WARMS A room, but gives it a natural focal point as well. And wood stoves, like wood-burning fireplaces, offer all the sense-enveloping sights, sounds, and smells that only burning logs provide. Unlike an open fireplace, however, a stove is an efficient heater, capable of serving as a primary heat source for one or more rooms.

Most wood-burning stoves are made of steel or cast iron. *(For more information on wood-burning soapstone stoves, see page 141.)* Steel stoves are generally less expensive than cast iron. Because they're most often designed to circulate heat, rather than simply radiate it, they may be a good choice for heating more than one room.

The thick body of a cast-iron stove holds the fire's heat, radiating warmth even after the flames have died out. Because of this radiating feature, they work best located away from a wall, allowing heat to move freely in all directions.

While it may be tempting to buy the biggest stove you can afford, it's important to keep in mind the size of the space you want to heat. A large stove can make a small room uncomfortably hot. Take your room and home dimensions with you when shopping for a stove, and ask the dealer to advise you on optimum stove size.

New wood-stove technology makes it possible to burn not only the wood, but also the gases and particles from the burning process that once

Make room for a stove in a small kitchen by creating a bumpout, *above.* A tiled niche also holds logs.

Surround a stove with rugged pine paneling, *right,* and fish-themed accessories to create a North Woods ambience.

Upgrading Options

simply went out the chimney, making stoves more efficient than ever. Look for convenience features such as top- or front-loading options and check to see that ash removal is easy.

A recent development to consider is the highly efficient pellet-burning stove. It uses a hopper to fuel the fire with small rounds of compressed sawdust and wood waste. The price tag is higher, but installation may cost a bit less. Because these stoves use electricity to operate the hopper, be sure they come with a backup battery to take over in a power outage.

An energy-efficient stove insert can be fitted into a heat-gobbling masonry fireplace, sending more heat out into the room and less up the chimney. Because the closed stove creates a hotter fire than an open fireplace, the existing chimney should be relined. Following the manufacturer's recommended clearances, choose a stove that's in scale with the firebox. Too small and it will seem lost; too large and it will look uncomfortably cramped.

Take a comfort cue from the
Europeans: Rather than heating the
whole house to the same temperature,
rely on stoves, *left,* to boost the heat in
whichever rooms are in use.

EuroStyle

IN THE SNOWY CLIMES OF Scandinavia and Northern Europe, where long winters reign and central heating was as uncommon as palm trees, masonry stoves remained a prime heating source through the mid-20th century. Flames hidden deep inside the stove warmed a series of inner chambers that held and transferred heat to tile exteriors which, in turn, sent out an even, comforting warmth.

Today's ceramic and soapstone stoves continue the tradition, with a notable change. Glass doors reveal the once-invisible flames, allowing for "fire-watching." For a primary heat source that yields constant warmth, a wood-burning masonry heater may be the answer.

The initial cost is high, both for the stove and the installation, which requires a sturdy foundation. But the highly efficient stove needs to be fired only once or twice a day. Large units, such as the soapstone stove, *right,* soak up enough heat from a two-hour fire to radiate warmth for up to 24 hours. Incorporating a baking oven lets the heat do double duty.

While American-made stoves often have nostalgic styling or a rugged profile that's clearly intended to look at home in a seaside cottage or mountain retreat, European styles, *left,* have unembellished, modern lines. More "sleek sports car" than "horse and buggy," they pair well with contemporary furnishings.

Stoves of this type heat by convection—circulating air—as well as radiation. Available in gas- or oil-burning models, the stoves tend to be highly efficient and clean-burning because of heightened attention to environmental issues in many European countries.

Adding a weighty soapstone or glazed tile stove, *right,* to
your home calls for on-site construction by expert installers
and attention to structural support.

Old-world styling combines with high-tech expertise to produce stoves that demand a second look.

FabulousFakes

CALL IT "STOVE-LITE," THE WOOD-FREE OPTION THAT GIVES YOU THE LOOK without the lugging. Manufacturers of gas and electric stoves continue to work more diligently than Santa's elves to produce increasingly authentic fires that match the appealing look of burning wood, while requiring no more effort on your part than the flick of a switch or the touch of a button.

Most log sets for both stoves and fireplaces are made of the same material: usually durable fiber-ceramic and sometimes concrete or other heat-resistant substances. The material is formed in molds made from real cord wood. The differences come in the attention given to the colors and texture of the logs' barklike exteriors. If realism is important to you, look for log sets that vary full and split pieces, and charred logs with those that appear untouched by

Establish a cottage feeling by tucking a nonworking antique stove, *below,* into a bedroom, family room, or home office. All the charm, no fuss.

The electric stove with a 3-D flame, *left,* means you stay toasty warm without chopping kindling or hauling out ashes.

fire. Birch and oak are favorites, but if you're truly persnickety, you may even want to track down log sets that resemble less common wood species native to your area.

Sets of artificial logs fit together in a particular pattern. You can choose among various configurations, depending on which overlapping design you find most appealing.

Manufacturers also vie to produce natural-looking flame patterns and add refinements that change the blue flame of natural gas to a cheery yellow. Often the logs sit on a base of lacy rock wool that resembles a bed of glowing embers.

Freestanding gas stoves must be vented, but electric stoves simply plug into the wall, using a standard 110-volt outlet. There's no venting—though you can add a vent, *left,* to complete the wood-stove illusion. The electric heater function operates independently of the simulated flame effect, so on warm days when you'd like to enjoy the look of a fire, you can have it with no heat. Because the unit is portable, you can move it to another room—or another home.

Antiques and flea-market enthusiasts may be lucky enough to find the real McCoy—a vintage wood-burning stove. Even if you're not interested in spending the money and effort to bring an old-timer back to working condition, you may want to consider using it as a charming accent piece. Give the surface a good cleaning and paint it an attractive color. An old stove's history and eye-catching shape make it a sure-fire conversation piece.

Finally, for those determined to complete the illusion of any fabulously fake stove or fireplace, it is possible to buy audiotapes of crackling, sputtering, hissing flames, and augment them with incense to enjoy the evocative aroma of pinecones tossed on a campfire.

You'll have to look twice to spot the fakes among these wannabe stoves and fireplaces that work hard to look like the real thing.

Don't leave your just-pretend fireplace with a blank expression. Accessories such as a sizable basket of flowers, *left,* soften the starkness of the opening and maintain the illusion of a working fireplace.

Sometimes, the time or place is just not right for a working fireplace. You may be renting, or living in an area or structure where local codes forbid fireplaces. But you don't have to give up the charm and architectural oomph a fireplace provides if you're willing to make do with a fabulous fake. Here are three routes to fireside sleight of hand:

Search for a vintage fireplace surround at flea markets, antique shops, and architectural salvage warehouses. Your job will be easier than it might be for someone who has an existing working fireplace that calls for a mantel of a certain size. Choose whatever style and size suit your budget and taste.

Check your home improvement center for packaged mantel kits. These ready-to-assemble projects come in a limited number of styles and sizes, but their ready-cut pieces and assembly instructions make them a convenient shortcut.

Find a fireplace style you like in a shelter magazine and duplicate it using individual molding pieces from the lumberyard or home improvement center. Add your own touches to take do-it-yourself to the creative level of design-it-yourself. The decorative elements of the fireplace, *above,* are attached to a base of mounting boards. Follow these steps:

- *Using a pencil and a level,* mark the locations for the pilasters' concealed mounting boards. Secure with 3-inch flathead screws or hollow-wall anchors.
- *Attach pilasters to mounting boards* by screwing through the sides. Attach the mantel by using a horizontal mounting board.
- *To finish,* caulk screw holes and cracks, then prime and paint moldings. Paint the wall inside the "firebox" a dark color to add depth.

Longing for a fireplace but not quite ready for a working model? Find fulfillment with a fool-the-eye version.

If you have an artistic streak, you may want to tackle the ultimate in virtual fireplaces—a trompe l'oeil version. A French phrase that means "fool the eye," trompe l'oeil refers to a painting that's so realistic, the viewer may be convinced, at least for a short time, that it's the real thing. Legend has it that the master of this technique was a Greek artist who painted grapes so lifelike, birds swooped down to try to eat them off the canvas.

For a true trompe l'oeil look, you may need to consult local art schools, perhaps galleries, or specialty paint stores to find someone who has mastered this technique. To create a version of this effect that doesn't require freehand artistic talent, consider using a stencil technique similiar to the one was used on the fireplace wall *below*.

Find a photo in a book or magazine of a fireplace you like. Using a photocopier, copy and enlarge the various details until you have the elements to make up a fireplace in a size that fits your space. Using these pieces as patterns, cut a series of stencils. (Your local hobby store can advise you on materials and techniques.)

Care and patience are the key to success in stenciling projects, along with high quality materials. Using professional-grade acetate sheeting for your stencils, for example, minimizes chances that paint will seep under the edges.

Hard as it may be to believe, not only the fireplace, but everything on this primly perfect fireplace wall, *left,* is two-dimensional, from the gold-framed picture to the brass andirons. Even the wallpaper background is skillfully painted, using custom-cut stencils. Note the use of subtle shadows along edges to add realism.

Rustic furnishings and sturdy fabrics, *above,* are good companions to the casual, sculptural charm of a clay chiminea.

THERE'S SOMETHING BOTH PRIMITIVE AND LUXURIOUS ABOUT AN OUTDOOR fire. Recently, various freestanding products that bring the camaraderie of a campfire and the romance of a full-blown fireplace to your back door have appeared. You can choose from hefty 6-foot-tall steel "fireplaces" meant to remain where you site them, to chubby 3-foot-tall R2D2-like models that can be wheeled wherever they're needed.

Terra-cotta chimineas are curvaceous stand-alone fireplaces inspired by traditional bread ovens used in Mexican villages. Strictly for heating, not baking, they consist of a clay body set in a metal stand. Some types have caps or screens to keep rain, debris, and small animals out when not in use. Chimineas range from about 2 to 4 feet tall. The diminutive ones are the right size for a balcony or other small space. More substantial

OutdoorFires

Like their indoor counterparts, gas-fueled outdoor fires, *left,* provide fireside atmosphere without the need to build and feed a fire.

These are a good choice if you'd like to buy a single product that you can use at home or take along to a beach or campsite.

Look for wood-burning products with exteriors that resist rusting and mesh sides that are fine enough to contain flying embers and sparks.

The fire in the lantern-like aluminum and stainless-steel outdoor hearth, *below,* doesn't come from wood. Instead, a gel-based alcohol fuel feeds flames that leap and crackle around fiber-ceramic logs. It's glass-enclosed rather than screened and disassembles for storage.

You'll find outdoor fireplace products at patio shops and home centers, as well as at fireplace dealers. Some gardening supply catalogs also feature stylish patio fireplace options.

ones look at home on a roomy patio. (The chiminea, *left*, was fitted with a venting pipe because of its porch placement.)

Other widely available wood-burning, outdoor hearth products include solidly built steel models in various configurations—round, square, tepee-shape—that enclose the fire with heavy-duty mesh sides. Doors swing open to allow access to the fire for those occasions when only a gooey, blackened marshmallow on a stick will satisfy.

Some small, wheeled models offer an optional grill that slips into place above the fire so the unit can do double duty as heater and cooker. Either wood or charcoal can be used for fuel.

Light up the night with an outdoor hearth that brings the cheer and charm of the campfire up to date.

If you face wood-burning restrictions, look for products such as this outdoor stove, *above,* which burns gel-alcohol fuel.

technical

information

Fireplace Options

THE INITIAL APPEAL OF A FIREPLACE is emotional, but actually getting to that warm, crackling fire and maintaining it requires a pragmatic approach. There are lots of choices and decisions to make, whether you're updating an existing fireplace or adding a new one.

Those choices and decisions will be much easier to make when you have a good understanding of your wants and needs. Answer the four key questions that follow, and you'll be ready to handle a barrage of options.

What do you want your fireplace to do? Provide heat for a room or create a cozy ambience—or both? Some types of fireplaces are efficient heaters. Wood stoves, for example, are very efficient sources of heat but create a rustic, rather than elegant, fireside atmosphere. Natural-gas-

fueled fireplaces are easy-care, efficient sources of heat and have the look of a traditional hearth or a stove.

What are your fuel source options? Wood, natural gas, or another source? First, check with your local building department. In some parts of the country, for instance, wood-burning fireplaces are restricted. Also, all fuel sources are not always available in every region.

The placement of a fireplace or stove within a house can affect fuel choice too. Add a new wood-burning fireplace, and you'll need to construct a chimney—that's costly. A direct-vent, natural gas fireplace may be perfect for a bedroom, but running a gas line through existing walls can be tricky.

Do you want a chimney? A few years ago, chimneys were a requisite part of a fireplace. Now, chimneys are a necessity only for wood-burning fireplaces

and stoves. Direct-vent gas units and some wood-pellet-burning units require a small opening on an exterior wall; electric, gel-fueled, and vent-free gas units require no external outlet.

How much maintenance work are you willing to do? Gas, electric, and gel-fueled stoves and fireplaces are simpler to maintain than wood-burning units. You want your fireplace to be a safe addition to your home. Whatever type of fireplace you have or choose to install, be sure to understand the maintenance required.

Read on for answers. The important information you need to make the best choices is all in this chapter. You'll also find sources here, making it easy to contact manufacturers and organizations involved in the hearth industry. With information at your fingertips, you'll be closer to the safe, romantic fireplace of your dreams.

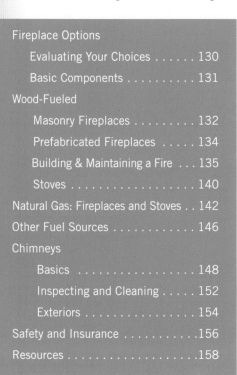

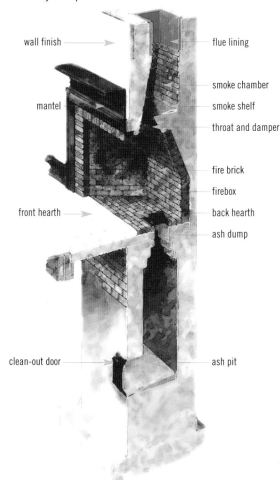

wall finish

flue lining

smoke chamber

mantel

smoke shelf

throat and damper

fire brick

firebox

front hearth

back hearth

ash dump

clean-out door

ash pit

Basic Components of a Fireplace

You'll find fireplaces in many shapes and sizes, yet they all share some basic elements. So no matter what type of fireplace you're considering, this page will serve as a reference to understand its construction and installation.

Since other types of fireplaces evolved from a masonry fireplace, *right*, it's a useful starting point for explaining components. Prefabricated fireplaces, for example, are similar except they're made mostly of metal and have no ash pit.

The firebox is the open area that contains the fire. In masonry fireplaces, the firebox is lined with firebrick, a type of masonry specially manufactured to withstand hot, intense fires. In prefabricated fireplaces, the firebox is lined with metal or a refractory material that looks like masonry bricks.

The hearth technically refers to the floor of the fireplace; the term is also used to refer to the entire fireplace. The *back hearth* is the bottom of the firebox. The *front hearth* extends a short distance into the living area and is usually decorative and made from brick, stone, or tile.

The throat is the area directly above the firebox and below the flue. This narrow opening allows the hot air and smoke to gain speed as they enter the flue, creating a draft that keeps the fire burning properly and prevents smoke from entering the room.

The damper is the moveable metal flap covering the throat; it's opened and closed manually. The open damper allows the fire to burn and smoke to escape. When the fire is out, the damper should be closed to prevent warm inside air from flowing up and out the chimney.

The smoke chamber is the space directly above the throat. This prevents downdrafts where outside air flows down into the firebox and causes smoke to flow into the room. Also, the smoke recirculates here so that particulates are thoroughly burned before going up the chimney. The flat bottom of the smoke chamber is called the *smoke shelf*.

The flue is the inside of the chimney. In today's fireplaces, flues are lined with heat-resistant, interlocking clay or ceramic tiles, insulated metal pipe, or cast-in-place, heat-resistant concrete. The liner protects the chimney walls from heat and corrosion. A cast-in-place concrete liner is especially effective for repairing older chimneys because it helps ensure the structural integrity of aged bricks and mortar.

A cap is installed at the top of the chimney. It keeps rain from entering the chimney where it mixes with soot to create acidic compounds that deteriorate the flue lining. A cap also helps to prevent downdrafts in particularly windy conditions. A cap should sit at least 12 inches above the end of the chimney opening. (Caps are not required by code; not every chimney has one.)

An ash pit, a chamber for collecting ashes located below the firebox, is found only on masonry fireplaces. Opening a small metal door in the floor of the firebox allows ashes to be swept into the ash pit. A *clean-out door* is located below the fireplace, often in the basement, for ash removal.

Chimney cap

Wood: Masonry Fireplaces

Shallow Rumford fireplaces, *above,* make a blaze visible from almost every point in the room.

IN COLONIAL TIMES, FIREPLACES were large—they had to be to heat entire homes and to accommodate big logs, often whole logs. A modern fireplace rarely bears the same responsibility for heating a whole house, yet its owner does face an age-old dilemma: finding the right balance of size and shape of the firebox, the size of the throat, and the height of the chimney, so that fires burn vigorously and smoke doesn't back up into rooms.

There are three basic configurations *(see page 133)* that characterize the design of the wood-burning, masonry fireplaces being built today:

☞ *The Rumford fireplace* is the forebear of the modern fireplace, and it is a favorite model for contemporary fireplace design. It is named for Count Rumford, a Massachusetts-born scientist whose 18th-century work was primarily concerned with the nature of heat. Rumford fireplaces have shallow fireboxes 18 to 20 inches deep, rounded throats, side walls angled at 45 degrees, and upright, vertical backs. The shallow firebox and angled side walls are designed to radiate more heat toward interior rooms, while the straight back allows smoke and gases to exit directly into the flue.

☞ *The Orton fireplace* is named after Vrest Orton, author of the 1969 book, *The Forgotten Art of Building a Good Fireplace.* Orton's design pitched the back wall of the firebox forward slightly to better reflect heat toward living spaces. Because the slanted back would sometimes allow smoke to drift into interiors, Orton compensated by creating a straight throat that ensured a powerful draw and eliminated smoke infiltration.

☞ *The modern fireplace* features a steeply pitched back wall and a throat positioned well forward of the flue.

Opening an Unused Fireplace and Chimney

A fireplace that hasn't been used for a while has not escaped the passage of time. If you've decided to rekindle the flames in an old fireplace, be sure to have it inspected, cleaned, and updated to ensure that it's safe to use. Hire a pro to do the job, and here's what you might find:

• Unused chimneys are quiet, safe places that appeal to birds, squirrels, or raccoons. You may have to evict some wildlife to clear the flue and repair any damage before the fireplace is usable. If the cap is screened, you may not have wildlife to worry about, but bugs, small birds or rodents, and debris may clog the chimney.

• An unused chimney is vulnerable to damage from the elements. Water and ice can damage the flue and the chimney exterior.

• Sometimes old chimneys are simply closed at the throat with a plug of brick or concrete to seal out drafts. Chipping out the plug can damage the flue lining, and the damper may need to be replaced.

• If the fireplace is unused in a house you're thinking of buying, ask why. Poor draw or a flue fire mean there are repairs you'll have to make before you can use the fireplace again.

• Installing a fireplace insert in an unused fireplace is a good way to improve the efficiency, plus, you'll have the opportunity to add some of the modern conveniences. *(For more information, see page 133.)*

Rumford

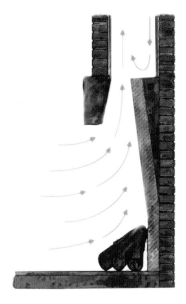

Orton

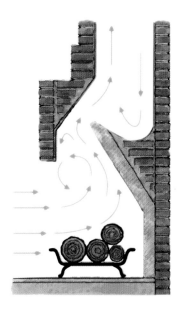

Modern

This design forces smoke and hot gases to rotate just before entering the flue, ensuring complete combustion inside the firebox and producing maximum heat. Generally, this design does not radiate heat into living spaces as effectively as the Rumford or Orton.

Adding a masonry fireplace involves a significant commitment in time and money. Expect to pay $6,000 to $8,000 for a no-frills brick fireplace featuring a 4 x 3-foot firebox opening and a 20-foot-tall chimney. The floor beneath the fireplace will have to be reinforced all the way to the foundation to bear the weight of the masonry, adding even more expense—and likely precluding putting one on the second story of a house.

Fireplace Inserts

If you have an older masonry fireplace and want some of the conveniences of modern fireplace design, a fireplace insert may be a good choice. An insert is a wood-burning or gas unit designed to fit into the opening of a traditional fireplace. Like a new fireplace or stove, an insert must meet strict EPA guidelines for combustion efficiency and pollution control.

Inserts are boxes made of cast iron or heavy-gauge steel with glass doors on the room-facing side to make the flames visible. They are made either to fit completely inside the existing masonry fireplace opening or to protrude slightly—a design that allows more heat to radiate into the room. A popular option is an electric blower that pulls in cooler room air, circulates it around the body of the insert, then blows the warmed air back into the room. An insert does not include a chimney system and must be connected to an existing chimney with a sealed collar. You may need a chimney liner to resize the flue.

Inserts are heavy, weighing 600 to 1,000 pounds. Installation should be done by a fireplace professional who is familiar with proper techniques. A top-quality insert will cost $1,200 to $2,000, depending on the size and the number of options selected.

Wood: Prefabricated Fireplaces

FACTORY-BUILT FIREPLACES LOOK LIKE traditional masonry even though they're made mostly of metal. These prefabricated units include a firebox, a chimney system, and all the necessary parts such as a damper and chimney cap. Often, these fireplaces include hook-ups for drawing outside air for combustion, a feature that makes them extremely energy efficient.

Because they are relatively light-weight—typically 300 to 500 pounds—and do not need the extensive foundation footings required for masonry fireplaces, prefab fireplaces can be installed on any floor of a home without reinforcing wood floor joists. They're a popular choice for adding fireplaces to existing homes and for building in new homes.

A Note of Caution
The firebox and chimney of a prefabricated unit are engineered to work together. A prefab firebox should not be attached to an existing chimney. Always follow the manufacturer's instructions and guidelines for installation.

These fireplace units sometimes are called zero-clearance fireplaces, meaning they can be installed close to wood framing members without creating a fire hazard. Depending on the type of fireplace, a gap as little as half an inch is sufficient to protect the framing—a fact that makes them ideal for retrofit situations.

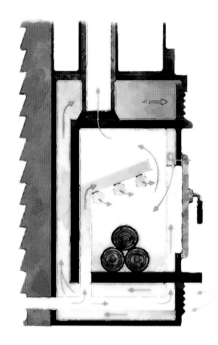

One advantage of a prefabricated fireplace is its low cost—for the unit and for the labor required to install it. Expect to pay $500 to $2,000, depending on the size and features of the model. Installation is easy compared to the process of building a masonry fireplace. Experienced contractors can install a prefabricated fireplace in as little as two days. Add $1,000 to $1,500 for installation.

The units come in standard sizes and have a set number of options for customizing the appearance of the opening. Get the size specifications from the manufacturer so that you allow the correct amount of space for the unit. Mantels, surrounds, and front hearth material, however, are generally not included in manufacturer's measurements. Leave room to create a custom look for your room.

To maximize efficiency, many prefabricated fireplaces, *left,* use outside air to feed the fire (the arrows that come in at the left on the bottom) and circulate room air around the firebox to distribute heat (shown as the arrows that start on the bottom right).

It's generally assumed that metal fireplaces are not as long-lasting as their more massive masonry counterparts due to the corrosive acids and water vapor produced during combustion. However, the prefabricated fireplace industry is not mature enough to judge the ultimate performance of these metal units over an extended period. Most manufacturers offer 30-year limited warranties on their products. To ensure peak performance and longevity from your prefabricated fireplace, inspect it each year for signs of deterioration.

Size Wise
Standard prefabricated fireplace units produce anywhere from 25,000 to 50,000 Btus. A fireplace that burns at 35,000 Btus can heat a 1,500-square-foot space, depending on location. A dealer can help you determine which fireplace is the right size for your home.

Wood: Building and Maintaining a Fire

ONE OF THE BEST WAYS TO KEEP A fireplace operating at peak efficiency is to build and maintain proper fires. The type of fire you create, the temperature at which it burns, and the kind of wood you use all affect the quantity and quality of fireplace emissions. Properly constructed fires burn cleanly and are less likely to produce creosote, the flammable, tar-like substance that can build up inside flue walls and ignite into a roaring chimney fire. Properly tended fires provide more heat, produce less creosote, and leave fewer ashes, reducing cleanup chores.

Choosing and Storing Firewood

Different kinds of wood have different burning and heating qualities. The type of heat produced varies with the density of the wood. Generally, firewood is available in three densities. **Hard or dense woods** produce an intense heat, burn for long periods of time, and leave little ash residue. Because dense woods are a more efficient fuel, they have the highest cost per cord. **Low-density woods** start readily and burn fast, but they burn at lower temperatures than dense woods—a factor that may allow creosote to build up on flue walls. **Medium-density woods** strike a balance between heating efficiency and cost (*see firewood chart, page 139*).

For maximum efficiency and to ensure your wood produces only a minimal amount of creosote, it must be dry or "seasoned." For this reason, buy wood in the spring and store it over the summer so that it dries out completely.

Store wood away from your house. Wood piles attract ants, termites, and other insects, as well as chipmunks and squirrels, and you don't want these pests trying to build nests in your siding or showing up in your pantry. Stack wood no more than two rows wide so that air circulates freely around all the pieces. Don't try to pack it too tightly—gaps help the wood dry out. Build a platform to keep the wood off the ground or simply sacrifice the bottom rows of your woodpile—because they are in contact with the ground, they will not dry out. To keep the stack from getting too elongated, drive stout stakes at the ends of each row to pile the wood against. When you're finished, cover the pile with a plastic drop cloth. Place a few chunks of wood on top of the drop cloth to hold it in place. The drop cloth should cover the top few layers but not the whole pile. That way, air will circulate among the pieces.

Keep a small supply of wood indoors for immediate use, so you don't have to head outdoors for more fuel during the middle of a fireside conversation. Many kinds of storage hoppers hold up to a dozen chunks of firewood at a time—usually enough for an evening's fire. Some fireplaces have nooks for holding firewood built into the masonry or hearth surround. If you like having

A handsome fireplace screen enhances a hearth's good looks while keeping flying sparks in their place. Glass doors go beyond adding a finished appearance and corralling wayward sparks to keeping your home's heat from going up the chimney when the damper is open. They're a handy safety measure too, allowing you to leave a fire unattended for a moment or two.

Standard glass doors come in arched and rectangular styles. Depending on the size and shape of your fireplace opening, you may need custom-fitted doors. Take your exact measurements along when you're shopping, adding a sketch if the opening is anything other than a rectangle. Clear glass allows the truest view of the fire, but if your concern is hiding the firebox when it's not in use, tinted and mirrored glass is available. Polished or antiqued brass frames and hardware are most common; to complement the style of your fireplace and room, you may want to consider nickel, chrome, copper, or basic black. If you have built-in cabinetry surrounding the fireplace, match the material of the screen frame to the door and drawer hardware. Contemporary fireplaces pair up well with frame-free glass doors with concealed hinges.

firewood in a hopper or storage bin for looks as well as for use, make sure that you use up all the wood periodically and restock with fresh wood. Empty your hoppers and bins every two weeks and sweep up the debris. That way, if your firewood is home to any wood-boring insect pests, they won't establish themselves in your house framing.

Hearth Accessories

Andirons, sometimes called firedogs, are paired metal supports used to keep firewood off the hearth floor so that air can circulate beneath the fire, creating a more efficient burn. Viewed from the side, andirons are L-shaped, with the lower portion supported by short legs. Seen from the front, the vertical members are highly decorative and serve to keep logs from rolling forward into the living area. More than a century ago, when hearths were used for cooking, andirons were used to support spits for roasting. New and antique andirons are available in a variety of styles to match interior decor.

Fireplace grates serve the same purpose as andirons—supporting firewood and allowing air circulation beneath the fire for maximum burning efficiency. Grates, however, are more functional than decorative and manufactured as ordinary steel or iron grids supported by four short legs. Grates are available in different widths and depths to accommodate different-size hearths. Some grates are heat exchangers made of hollow, tubular steel. With the assistance of a fan, room air is circulated through the tubes so that it can be heated. The warmed air is then blown back into the room.

Fireplace screens, made of fine steel mesh and designed to prevent flying sparks and embers from entering living areas, come in three types. **Folding screens** have three hinged panels and are placed in front of the fireplace opening. **Standing screens** are single-piece units and feature a metal frame supported by legs. Standing screens usually have decorative scrollwork that makes them attractive accessories when the fire is out. **Curtain screens** are installed along the top edge of the fireplace opening. The two halves of the screen are opened and closed by means of a pull chain, much like window drapery. When buying a curtain screen, it should be sized to fit the width of the hearth with enough screen material to create undulating folds in the screen when the curtains are pulled shut.

Accessories, such as andirons, *left,* are available at many stores, from specialty shops to major retailers.

If you're building or refurbishing a fireplace, consider including a niche, *left,* for firewood.

Tools

Fireplace tools are sold as sets that include a long-handled brush, a shovel, and a poker. Each tool is about 28 inches long and features a fireproof metal shaft. Sets include a convenient stand that can be placed close to the hearth. Use the **brush and shovel** to clean ashes from the hearth floor only after the fire is completely out and the ashes are cold. The **poker** has a handle with a short prod and a backward facing hook at the "business end" to manipulate and rearrange burning firewood.

Sets are available in a black matte finish or polished brass.

Fireplace tongs use a scissors action to grip pieces of wood. They are invaluable for rearranging firewood while fires are burning and for capturing and replacing logs that have fallen out of the burning pile. Made of heavy steel or iron, fireplace tongs are no doubt the most practical and

Old copper boilers, *below,* make perfect indoor firewood storage containers. You'll find them at flea markets and antique shops.

indispensable of the various fire-tending tools.

Slings of sturdy canvas or polyester duck are used to carry firewood from the woodpile to the fireplace. These rectangular pieces of fabric have handles at both ends and reinforced edge bindings. They are easily folded for storage.

Improving Fireplace Performance

There are several ways to get more usable heat from your wood-burning fireplace. Warm-ducts circulate room air inside the fireplace core, where the air is heated by proximity to the firebox. The heated air then leaves the duct system and reenters the room. A passive warm-duct system pulls in cool air from near the floor, warms it, and allows it to leave by natural convection through vents placed near the upper portions of the fireplace. Mechanically assisted systems use fans to pull in room air.

Heat-exchanger fireplace grates are hollow. They use a fan to pull in room air, heat it, and blow it back out toward the room. Because the grates are so close to the fire, the air is heated quickly and thoroughly.

Glass doors serve several purposes. They keep sparks and hot debris from falling into the room area. Vents at the bottom of the doors limit the amount of room air drawn by the fire, preventing excess loss of room heat. Glass doors can be shut as the fire dies out, preventing warm room air from escaping up the chimney.

Tips on Buying Wood

Buy firewood in the spring to give it a chance to dry out or "season" thoroughly before using it.

Firewood is sold by the cord—128 cubic feet of neatly stacked wood. The standard cord is a pile of wood 4 feet wide, 4 feet high, and 8 feet long. Insist on measuring the amount of wood you are about to purchase. Multiply the three dimensions to make sure you are buying a full cord.

Don't buy wood that is described as a rack, face cord, or truckload. These are undefined terms and their use for advertising purposes is even prohibited in some states.

Buy wood split to no larger than 4–6 inches in diameter. The wood seller should have done most of the splitting work for you and included the labor cost in the price of a cord. Also, make sure the price of the cord includes stacking it in a location of your choosing, not just delivered to the end of your driveway.

In many states, firewood vendors are required to provide an invoice that shows the seller's name, address, contact phone numbers, and the total price of the wood purchased.

Using Firelogs

Firelogs are made of sawdust mixed with petroleum wax. They were invented in the 1960s as a way to

---

Maximizing the Draw

The notion of a crackling fire burning on a chilly winter's evening may be romantic and comforting, yet fireplaces are not necessarily efficient sources of heat. In many fireplaces, most of the heat generated goes straight up the chimney. Also, fires require air, and lots of it. Fireplace combustion takes air from indoor rooms and replaces it with air from outdoors, pulling it in through cracks around windows and doors. That's why when a fireplace is burning bright, nearby rooms may feel colder than usual, even with your home's heating system set at normal temperatures.

Paradoxically, today's energy-efficient houses tend to make matters worse. Modern construction products—tightly sealed windows, high-tech weatherstripping, and exterior house wraps—stop heat loss and prevent unwanted air infiltration, but can starve fireplace fires. The result is often poor draw, smoky rooms, and cool-burning fires that deposit creosote on flue walls. In worst-case scenarios, starved fires draw air through the only sources available—from exhaust pipes that vent gas-burning appliances to the outside. When that happens, dangerous amounts of carbon monoxide can be pulled back into the house.

If you suspect a lack of air is causing poor combustion in your fireplace, experiment by opening a window a couple of inches. Select a window located in the same room as the fireplace. If this helps, you probably need an outside air kit—a small vent that installs directly into your wall. Outside air kits have screened openings on the outside that prevent insects from entering the vents and air filters to remove dust and pollen. The inside cap is about the same size as a common smoke alarm. Drawing air through an outside air kit prevents your fireplace from pulling air in through cracks at windows and doors, resulting in warmer rooms throughout the house—an especially helpful feature for older homes. For maximum efficiency, the kit should be located in the same room as the fireplace.

When the fireplace works no better with a window open than closed, the problem may lie in the design. The opening of the fireplace and the size of the chimney flue must be in the correct proportion to create good draw. Ideally, the area of the opening should be 12 times larger than the interior diameter of the flue. Hire a fireplace professional to determine how to correct the situation.

Sometimes the culprit is the chimney: It may be too short and need to be extended. Although results aren't guaranteed and the work is expensive, this method will usually produce good results. Consult with a professional mason who has experience building fireplaces.

Wood Species	Density (lbs. per cubic ft.)	Btus (per cord in millions)
Hickory	50.9	27.7
Apple	48.7	26.5
White Oak	47.2	25.7
Sugar Maple	44.2	24
Red Oak	44.2	24
Yellow Birch	43.4	23.6
White Ash	43.4	23.6
Cherry	36.7	20
Elm	35.9	19.5
Soft Maple	34.4	18.7
Douglas Fir	32.2	18.2
Norway Pine	31.4	17.1
Hemlock	29.2	15.9
Ponderosa Pine	28	15.2
Aspen	27	14.7
White Pine	26.3	14.3
Cottonwood	24.8	13.5
Basswood	24.8	13.5

recycle waste sawdust. Firelogs are often sold as individually wrapped logs and require no kindling or other starting material; they can be lit with a single match. Firelogs burn steadily and leave little ash. They're a convenient alternative to cord wood, especially for the homeowner who lights a fire only occasionally throughout the year. However, they are considerably more expensive and aren't recommended for wood stoves.

Studies conducted by the Oregon Department of Energy indicate that firelogs are a cleaner source of fireplace heat than natural cord wood, producing less particulates and carbon monoxide.

Building and Keeping a Fire

Start by making sure the damper is open and the firebox is free of old ashes. Leftover ashes may impede air flow and reduce your fire's ability to burn efficiently. With the grate centered in the firebox, crumple two or three sheets of newspaper and stuff them under the grate. Place pencil-

diameter kindling over the newspaper but on top of the grate. Crisscross the kindling to create air spaces all around the fuel—packed kindling will not burn properly. Over the kindling, place 1- to 2-inch-diameter pieces of wood, again in a crisscross pattern. You'll want to get this stack of wood going before adding larger chunks of firewood—placing bigger pieces now may disrupt your carefully constructed kindling pile.

With the damper open, place your hand near the throat of the flue and check for air movement. Downward movement or no movement at all probably means that the flue is cold and needs to be warmed. Twist two or three sheets of newspaper into a cone. Using the narrow end as a handle, light the larger end and hold it near the throat of the flue. The resulting updraft should pull smoke and flame up into the flue. Be careful handling the lit newspaper.

When the cone has burned halfway down, use it to ignite the newspapers under the grate. Once all the wood has started to burn with a vigorous flame, add larger pieces, again placing them in a crisscross pattern to facilitate air flow.

Once the fire is going well, add cord wood, two or three pieces at a time. Keep the fire burning vigorously. If the fire is allowed to die down to coals and smolder that way for long periods, it will burn at temperatures cool enough to allow creosote to form on the inside of flue walls. Always have an active flame on your fire. Use a fire screen to protect nearby surfaces from flying sparks and embers.

Never pour water on your fire to extinguish it—the extreme change in temperature may crack the firebox. Instead, allow a fire to die out naturally. Until it is completely out, don't close the damper. If you must leave a blazing fire unexpectedly, smother it with baking soda, sand, or cat litter.

Never leave a fire unattended.

Scrap the Scrap Lumber

Resist the temptation to use construction "leftovers" such as plywood, oriented-strand board, and deck lumber in your fireplace. The same is true for painted and stained wood. These materials contain toxic chemicals that are released into the air when the wood is burned. Skip digging through scrap lumber and stick to seasoned firewood for safety.

Wood: Stoves

The "parlor stove," *above*, is reminiscent of what you'd find in a Victorian home, but it burns modern wood pellets for efficient heating.

IF YOU WANT MAXIMUM HEATING from a wood-fired appliance, consider a freestanding wood stove. Today's models are much more energy-efficient than they were just a few years ago, thanks to strict particle-emissions standards imposed by the Environmental Protection Agency (EPA). Before EPA standards were implemented throughout the industry, most of the heat from wood stoves went out the stovepipe, along with smoke and other pollutants. Now, wood stoves sold in this country must be EPA certified, meaning that most of the fuel is completely consumed, producing heat that radiates into living spaces. This efficient combustion also burns up pollutants that otherwise would enter the atmosphere. Any wood stove you purchase should have a permanent notice of EPA certification attached to the back of the stove.

The same notice should carry a Btu rating for the stove. Be sure to select a rating that is compatible with the amount of space you intend to heat with your stove—your dealer should advise you. A common—and potentially dangerous—mistake is to select a stove with too high of an output. The problem is not the amount of heat that a powerful stove might generate, but the fact that in an effort to lower heat output, a homeowner would close down dampers and vents to keep fires burning low and slow, a condition that could lead to creosote build-up within the stovepipe (*see Quick Reference Terms, page 137*). To prevent creosote from forming, fires should be small, vigorous, and hot.

Look for a stove made of plate steel or cast iron at least ¼-inch thick. Better models have a "window-wash" feature. They are engineered to ensure that air blows across the inside face of glass doors to keep them free of soot. Choose a reputable manufacturer offering a limited lifetime warranty against defects. Ask people who own stoves for their recommendations, or inquire with chimney sweeps about their favorite brands.

Catalytic and Noncatalytic Stoves

Wood stoves certified by the EPA generally employ one of two techniques to ensure clean and efficient combustion. During normal operation, the internal temperatures of older, uncertified wood stoves aren't hot enough to ignite many of the byproducts of combustion. This is because some particulates and gases don't burn completely until temperatures are in excess of 1,000° F. However, a stove with a catalytic combustor reduces this burning point to about 600° F and encourages

Stove Sense

If you have a wood-burning stove that hasn't been used in a while and you'd like to put it back in service, do a little maintenance first.

• In addition to a chimney and stovepipe inspection and cleaning, inspect the joints in the firebox. The caulk in these joints deteriorates over time and needs to be inspected and replaced regularly. The same applies to the gasket around the door opening.

• The safety standards for wood-burning stoves and installation requirements have been updated since many older wood-burning stoves were installed. For example, the use of fireproof materials on surfaces surrounding woodstoves is now required. Check with the local building department to ensure your stove is in compliance, or check with your insurance agent.

complete combustion of available fuel. The results are longer, hotter fires, more radiant heat per cord, and fewer pollutants that reach the environment. A catalytic combustor needs occasional cleaning and lasts two to three years.

A noncatalytic stove has a heavily insulated firebox that retains and concentrates heat, allowing more complete combustion of byproducts. There is also a secondary combustion chamber that circulates smoke and gases under high heat, burning off particulates and other pollutants.

Using a Wood Stove

It's a good idea to have your wood stove installed by a professional so that all clearances and the stovepipe meet all regulations specified by your local building codes and fire protection ordinances, and so proper materials are used to protect nearby surfaces. If you are unsure about installation procedures, ask your local fire or building department for an inspection of your property and

advice about where and how to install a wood stove safely. For safety and efficiency while using your wood stove, follow these guidelines:

Remove ashes regularly. If ashes pile up on the floor of the stove, they can clog air-intake vents.

Don't overstoke fires. Before wood ignites, it absorbs energy. The energy required to ignite many pieces of wood cools down the overall temperature in the firebox, resulting in more smoke and pollutants. Instead, keep fires smaller and hotter by tending them often and using only seasoned wood.

Today's cast-iron stoves, *left,* have many benefits: old-fashioned charm, new-age efficiency, and fresh color choices.

Consider installing a stack thermometer in your stovepipe. A stack thermometer reads the internal temperature of stove combustion at a point just above the firebox. For best efficiency, try to keep temperatures about 350° F to 400° F.

Don't burn household garbage or other kinds of refuse. Some plastics and paints contain harmful chemicals that can be released into the air. Burning materials other than regular cord wood can damage catalytic combustors.

Have a chimney sweep examine your stove and stovepipe once each year to check them for defects and to keep them free of creosote. *(See Hiring a Chimney Sweep, page 149.)*

Fireplace-Stove Combinations

One of the best characteristics of a fireplace is the cozy ambience of the hearth. For a wood stove, it's heating efficiency. A fireplace-stove combination is a prefabricated unit that has the best of both. Combination fireplaces feature airtight doors and manually operated air vents, and they must meet standards set by the EPA for efficient particulate emissions.

What makes these units special is their mass—combination units weigh between 2,500 and 10,000 pounds and are composed mostly of brick, stone, and heat-resistant concrete block. The surrounding masonry is integral to the heating capabilities of the unit. Vents pull in outside air, heat it in a heat exchanger, then channel it through ducts running through the masonry. The heated masonry mass then releases warmth to interiors, providing a slow and steady source of heat, even after the fire has gone out. These units also have the capability to provide heat to other rooms through fan-assisted ducts. Outside air used for combustion ensures high heating efficiency.

A combination unit requires substantial structural reinforcement to support its weight. Some versions are freestanding and designed to be a prominent feature of room decor. Some are clad in soapstone, a material with exceptional heat-retention qualities that makes them efficient, elegant, and expensive. Expect to pay $5,000 to $20,000 for a fireplace-stove combination.

Natural Gas: Fireplaces and Stoves

IF YOU LIKE THE WARMTH AND ambience of a toasty fire in the fireplace but don't enjoy gathering wood, making fires, and cleaning out ashes, a gas-fired fireplace or stove or a gas log set may be a good choice for you. These choices are clean-burning, safe, and more energy-efficient than traditional wood-burning fireplaces.

One of the biggest advantages of gas-fired appliances is that they can be shut off completely and instantly when needed. Wood fires, on the other hand, usually are left to go out slowly and naturally. As they do, open

Direct-vent and vent-free gas fireplaces leave the mantel, *above,* unencumbered by a chimney, allowing more creative architecture such as an arched niche.

dampers permit indoor warmth to go up the chimney.

Today's gas fireplaces are engineered to provide more available heat than units manufactured just a few years ago. Some types are designed with thermostat controls, heat exchangers, and low-noise blowers that deliver hot air through ducts to rooms throughout the house.

Some gas-fired fireplaces include air-conditioning coils.

Fireplaces and Stoves

Gas-fired appliances come in two basic styles. Fireplace-like products include a traditional fireplace opening, hearth surround, and mantel. Stoves are freestanding units made of plate steel or cast iron and are supported on legs.

Both types typically feature fireproof ceramic logs placed on grates over realistic ceramic embers or beds of sand. Tiny holes in the logs and the embers emit gas that burns and creates random flame patterns to mimic the look of wood-fueled fires. Some stove units have ceramic burners that mimic coal-burning fires.

Newer gas fireplace appliances produce enough heat to be used as a supplemental heating source and are easily installed—making them ideal for retrofit situations. For example, it is possible to wall off the corner of a room, install a moderate-size gas fireplace in the wall cavity, and finish the wall to match the rest of the room in two or three days.

Fuel is provided by extending a gas line to the installation location. Another option is to convert an existing wood-burning fireplace by extending a gas line to the fireplace and installing a gas-burning fireplace insert or a set of ceramic logs. The extension of a gas line often is a simple operation if your fireplace is on the first floor. It can get tricky, however, if you're converting or adding a fireplace on an upper floor and have to run the line through existing walls.

Direct-Vent and Vent-Free

Whether you choose the old-fashioned look of a Franklin stove or the sleek style of a contemporary gas fireplace design *(see gas fireplaces and stoves, page 142)*, gas-fueled appliances can be purchased with direct vents or vent free.

Direct vents exhaust gases to the outside via a single vent. The vent does not need to go vertically through the roof, like a chimney. Instead, a short section of horizontal pipe exits through a wall. The same vent may contain an inner sleeve that draws in fresh air to be used for combustion. These types of gas-fired units don't require indoor air for burning and are highly energy-efficient. Direct-vent fireplaces can be fitted with traditional masonry or wood surrounds and vented glass doors.

As the name implies, *vent-free* units do not require venting for safe operation. The burners are designed to reduce carbon monoxide during combustion, allowing them to be installed virtually anywhere. Although these units meet all federal safety and emissions standards, some states restrict or

Direct-vent gas fireplaces, *above,* use double-walled pipe to supply air for the fire and to vent combustion gases (follow the arrows at the top of the illustration). A completely separate set of vents circulates and warms the indoor air (follow the arrows at lower right).

ban their use. Many states do not allow them to be used in bedrooms if the heating output exceeds 10,000 Btus per hour. In other states, these units aren't allowed in commercial buildings, motor homes, and bathrooms.

Check your local building department for any restrictions that apply in your area. Concerns include the use of these stoves in small rooms or virtually airtight locations, where they may deplete oxygen to unsafe levels. For safety, manufacturers of these appliances include an oxygen-depletion sensor—a switch that shuts off the appliance if oxygen falls below safe levels. Another concern is moisture. A vent-free appliance can produce a quart of water vapor per hour. To prevent unwanted condensation, a vent-free fireplace or stove should be

Using Propane

In many areas of the country, especially rural locations, propane (LP) gas may be the more practical—or only—choice to fuel gas-fired appliances. Propane has a slightly higher heat value than natural gas, but it costs more. It also requires a storage tank to store the gas near your home. Most gas appliances will work well with propane instead of natural gas, but the gas valves and burners must be properly sized and rated, and the unit must include a safety pilot light. Always check with your appliance dealer to make sure your equipment is correctly set up for burning propane fuel.

properly sized to the room or area where it is installed. If an excess-moisture problem persists, use a portable dehumidifier.

Gas Appliance Types

Direct-vent and vent-free gas appliances are made in several variations:

A vented gas fireplace insert is designed to convert a traditional, wood-burning fireplace into one that burns gas. The unit consists of an enclosed metal burning chamber that slides into an existing fireplace opening. Exhaust gases are vented out the chimney via a vent pipe. Fresh air for combustion is provided by room air, by a vent that penetrates an exterior wall and draws air directly into the burning chamber from outside, or by an exhaust vent that draws fresh air through an inner sleeve. These units often feature heat-resistant glass doors for viewing the flames. An average price is $1,400 to $1,800.

Vent-free inserts are also available for converting an existing wood-burning fireplace to gas. Because these units don't require ventilation, the installation labor cost is less than a direct-vent unit. Expect to pay between $1,000 and $1,200 for a vent-free insert.

Vented gas stoves, freestanding units made of metal that look like wood-burning stoves, vent exhaust through nearby walls. The entire unit radiates heat to the room, so these units are extremely energy-efficient. A quality direct-vent gas stove will cost $1,500 or more.

Gas logs are a low-cost option for converting a wood-burning fireplace to natural gas. These realistic replicas of wood fires feature ceramic logs created in many styles, wood species, and configurations. Gas logs come as either vented or vent-free models for $200 to $400. Vented models tend to have better-looking flames, but they consume more fuel per hour than vent-free types. Vent-free units produce more usable heat because all the heat is retained within the living space. Leave the job of converting from wood to gas to a licensed gas fitter and apply for a building permit, if needed in your area.

Once converted, the fireplace must be used exclusively for gas-fueled fires. For vented units, the fireplace damper must be in the open position when burning. The damper can

Matched Sets

The log sets in natural gas fireplaces can be unbelievably realistic—or abominably unrealistic. Either way, you're probably stuck with them once they're installed: Logs are most often configured as part of the system. For many models, you can't change the type of logs, and you can't change the placement of logs. Some systems are more flexible. Ask about changing the logs or the configuration before you buy.

The same goes for adjusting the flames. Some gas fireplace systems are simply on-off. Others allow variability—including the ability to vent up to 70 percent of the heat out the chimney, allowing you to have flames and glowing embers without overheating the room. If this feature appeals to you, check the model you're interested in to be sure this is an option.

Look for gas logs, *above,* placed in a pleasing, balanced arrangement with glowing embers and a well-hidden gas pipe.

remain closed for vent-free models. For both kinds, fireplace doors or air-control vents must remain open during burning.

Options

Gas-fired appliance manufacturers have taken advantage of electronic technology to offer a variety of sophisticated options. Many companies offer infrared, point-and-click remote controls, similar to television controls, that allow the user to switch flames on and off from across a room or to vary the height of the flames from flickering fires to roaring blazes. Some of the most imaginative controls employ computer technology that allows the user to program the type and duration of a fire, letting a vigorous fire burn down to glowing coals over a period of two or three hours.

Originally, the flame on a gas-fired appliance, like that on its wood-burning counterpart, matched its heat output: To get less heat, the flames had to be reduced. Now you'll find models that vent out excess heat so you can have high flames without overheating the room.

Care

Annual inspection and cleaning of the firebox and chimney are recommended to ensure the system is working correctly and to prevent problems.

The glass on a gas unit is designed to withstand the heat. If it cracks, don't use the unit until the glass is replaced and the unit has been inspected and approved for use.

Other Fuel Sources

THE HEARTH PRODUCTS INDUSTRY IS continually researching and developing new products, and every year refinements and improvements are made to existing lines of fireplaces, wood stoves, and accessories. Before deciding on what type of heating appliance you'd like in your home, be sure to look at the variety of alternative products available. Knowing what these units look like, what they burn, their heating ability, and how much they cost will allow you to make informed decisions about what kind of fireplace product is right for your home.

Pellet Stoves and Inserts

Pellet fuel is made from recycled sawdust compressed under great pressure to form hard nuggets about the size of small marbles. Pellets are inexpensive and easily stored. Typically, they are available in 40-pound bags. When burned, pellet fuel produces flames similar to cord wood. However, pellets burn with greater efficiency and produce less smoke and soot than traditional wood fires.

Appliances that burn pellet fuel are available as freestanding wood stoves and fireplace inserts. Both versions use an electric mechanism to deliver the pellets to the burning chamber at a rate determined by a thermostat. Some models can burn for days on a single load of pellets, reducing maintenance and fire-tending chores. Most pellet stoves and inserts are so efficient that they do not require a chimney and can simply be vented through a nearby wall to the outside. They also feature mechanical air-supply systems that use electric fans to control the amount of air entering the combustion chamber and to help expel the exhaust fumes. Expect to pay between $1,200 and $2,000 for a quality pellet-burning appliance.

One drawback of this type of heating appliance is the availability of pellets. If you'd like your stove or insert to serve as a supplemental heating source for your home, be sure to establish a reliable source of pellet fuel before purchasing your unit.

Coal-Burning Appliances

Anthracite coal burns cleanly and efficiently, producing almost no

A bayed pellet stove insert, *left,* efficiently sends heat into the room and creates a fire that's enjoyable to view.

The following table gives typical heating values for various appliances, expressed as a percentage of the total heat generated that is returned to the surrounding interiors.

Traditional wood fireplace	10 percent
Non-EPA certified wood stove or fireplace insert	35 percent
EPA-certified wood stove or fireplace insert	75 percent
Vented gas fireplace logs	10 percent
Direct-vent gas fireplace	40 percent
Direct-vent gas stove	75 percent
Vent-free fireplace, stoves, and logs	90 percent
Coal-burning stove	70 percent

smoke or creosote. It is usually burned in freestanding stoves designed to burn coal exclusively or made to burn either coal or wood. A coal-burning stove produces a long-lasting, even heat on a single load of fuel. Because there is little danger of producing creosote, the heat of a coal-burning appliance can be controlled effectively by regulating the amount of air, allowing the appliance to be "stopped down" to lower heat. However, coal stoves should never be allowed to run "full blast" for extended periods—the excess heat may destroy internal stove components.

The byproducts of coal combustion include sulphur compounds that deteriorate metal surfaces. Coal-burning stoves should be inspected at least once each year to check for any corrosion of metal surfaces. Before purchasing a coal-burning stove, you should find a reliable source of high-grade fuel coal in your area.

Electric Fireplaces and Inserts

Electric fireplaces run on standard household current and are ideal for retrofit situations or for apartments, condominiums, and other locations where wood- or gas-burning appliances are not allowed. Like standard fireplaces, they feature hearth surrounds and mantels, and many of the new units feature imitation flames that sway and flicker similar to a real fire. Lightweight wood-stove-style units are also available.

Some styles feature separate heating elements and flames, so you can use the unit as a space heater without

displaying flames, or display flames without heating the room. If you plan to use the unit as a space heater, be sure to get a model with variable heat settings to maintain a comfortable temperature.

Prices range from $500 to $3,000, depending on the size of the unit and the complexity of the hearth surround and mantelpiece.

Gel Fuel

For a low-maintenance, occasional evening fire, gel fuel fireplaces provide a good option. These freestanding units require no chimney or external outlet.

Sold as a complete unit, these fireplaces are fueled by cans of a solid fuel that's similar to the alcohol-based fuel often used under buffet serving dishes and fondue pots. Decorative logs hide the fuel can, and holes in the log spread the flame to almost the full width of the firebox. Remember that since these are real flames, you must heed all the precautions of having an open fire.

The hearth options include traditional and modern styles in a variety of colors, and wall and corner units. As with electric fireplace units, gel fuel fireplaces are a good choice for apartments, condominiums, and retrofit situations. The fireplace units run $300 to $800. The fuel costs about $3.50 per can; each can of fuel burns two to three hours.

Chimneys: Basics

ALL WOOD-BURNING FIREPLACES and stoves, as well as many natural gas units, require a chimney.

The chimney is the escape route for the unwanted byproducts of fire: carbon dioxide, smoke, and water vapor, and in some cases carbon monoxide and nitrous oxide. *(Many natural gas units need a vent in addition to a chimney. More information, see pages 142-145.)*

Not just any chimney, however, will do for every fireplace or stove. All chimneys should be lined—chimneys more than 50 years old may not be—and sized for the type and size of fireplace or stove in the house and for the distance to the outside. A liner of the wrong size or material can allow all the hot, air-borne crud and fumes to cool before they reach

Relining a Chimney

Because chimney flues typically are narrow and access is restricted, relining a chimney system can be a difficult and expensive job. Expect to pay between $150 and $200 per running foot to reline your chimney. If repairs are necessary, check with your insurance agent to see if your homeowner's policy covers a portion of the cost.

There are two basic methods of relining. In most cases, a round, insulated metal pipe, similar to the chimney pipe used for prefabricated fireplace units and wood-burning stoves, is inserted into the chimney. Any space between the pipe and the inside of the chimney is filled with a heat-resistant, fireproof plaster. Because the size of the throat and the smoke chamber is usually critical to combustion efficiency, the pipe may be held back from the lower portion of the chimney and the smoke chamber parged—coated with refractory cement.

A second method is to insert a form, usually a large vinyl or rubber hose, into the chimney. The hose is inflated to the proper diameter and the space between the hose and the interiors of the chimney walls is filled with lightweight, fireproof cement. Once the cement is set, the hose is deflated and removed. Although cast-in-place cement is not rated as a structural element, it is effective at helping preserve the structural integrity of older chimneys and aging mortar.

the chimney cap, causing them to fall back into the firebox and vent into your home, creating a potential health hazard.

A chimney should be sized in both diameter and length to match the fireplace or stove. This information is provided with new units, and a dealer can get the information for you if you're changing an existing unit. Here's a rundown on the basics to help you compare:

⇨ *Wood-burning stoves*, inserts, and prefabricated fireplaces burn at high temperatures—around 1,700° F—and require vertical flues able to withstand intense heat. A key word here is *vertical*; the chimney of any wood-burning appliance should exit the roof in as straight a line as possible, with as few angles as possible.

⇨ *Pellet stoves* burn cooler, requiring narrower flues that can be vented either through the roof or through a nearby wall.

⇨ *Natural gas firelogs* and fireplaces generate a lot of water vapor. Keeping condensation to a minimum is key, and a flue lining of stainless steel or aluminum is necessary. The venting requirements depend on the type chosen. (*See Natural Gas Fireplaces and Stoves, pages 142-145.*)

If you change the fuel source or the size or type of the firebox—

Hiring a Chimney Sweep

If you prefer to leave the messy chore of inspecting and cleaning your fireplace to someone else, hire a professional chimney sweep. Look in the Yellow Pages of your telephone directory under "Chimney Cleaning." For $100 to $140, a sweep will give your fireplace and chimney a thorough cleaning and check it for defects. Some sweeps lower video cameras and lights into chimneys to provide a close look at walls and liner surfaces and to establish a visual record of the chimney's condition for the homeowner. Many sweeps are qualified to complete necessary repairs or will recommend a professional masonry contractor to do the job.

The chimney sweep industry is not regulated or licensed by a government agency, but many sweeps apply for certification by the Chimney Safety Institute of America (CSIA) or membership in The National Chimney Sweep Guild (NCSG). These organizations promote professionalism in the industry by testing applicants and offering continuing education opportunities to keep members up-to-date on changing technology and fire safety. For more information and to find a qualified chimney sweep in your area, call the CSIA at 800/536-0118, or visit the website at www.csia.org. Visit the NCSG at www.ncsg.org.

converting from wood to gas, for example—make sure the chimney is in good shape and that the flue liner is the right size, material, and configuration for the new unit. *See Relining a Chimney, page 148*, for an idea of what's involved, but remember that this is a job that leaves no room for guesswork. Hire a professional to evaluate the chimney and to make any necessary repairs or install any replacement materials.

Installing a new fireplace or stove with a new chimney is more straightforward, and some new types of flue liners simply snap together. A capable do-it-yourselfer may be able to install a prefabricated fireplace and flue. Building the chimney, however, may be a bigger job than the average homeowner wants to put on the agenda.

For information on caring for chimneys, see *Chimneys: Inspecting and Cleaning, pages 152-153*, and *Chimneys: Exteriors, pages 154-155*.

Inspecting Your Fireplace

FIREPLACES AND CHIMNEYS SHOULD be inspected annually. Potential hazards such as chimney fires can be avoided with an annual inspection, conscientious fireplace upkeep, and an understanding of the best ways to build and maintain fires in the hearth.

As wood burns, it produces water vapor, gases, and unburned particulates: smoke. In a chimney that is clean and free of obstructions, these byproducts are quickly vented through the flue to the outdoors. However, as warm vapors reach the upper parts of the chimney they may encounter cooler air and condense, forming creosote, a black or brown residue that clings to the inner surfaces of the flue liner. This is especially true if fires are not burning at high enough temperatures—for example, if the fire is allowed to smolder and smoke, if wet wood is used, or if wood with an inherently low burning temperature, such as pine, is used regularly. *(See Building and Maintaining a Fire, pages 135-139.)*

Creosote is a highly flammable substance that comes in many forms. It can be hard and glassy, tarlike and sticky, or dry and flaky. If creosote is allowed to build up, it may catch fire. Flue liners for residential use must be certified by Underwriters Laboratories, an independent product-testing and safety agency, to

withstand temperatures of 1,700 ° F. However, a flue fire can reach 2,500° F. These high temperatures can crack brick, stone, or clay flue liners, allowing heat to reach nearby wood framing members and other combustible materials, such as insulation.

The best way to prevent flue fires is to make sure the flue is free of creosote. Inspect your chimney once a year. Late spring or early summer is a good time, when heating season is over. If you wait until fall, you may not have enough time to complete any necessary repairs before the heating season begins again.

Making an inspection yourself is not difficult, but prepare to get dirty. Wear old clothes—including a hat—and equip yourself with a dust mask or respirator and a pair of safety goggles. First, check the firebox for damage or cracks. In a masonry fireplace, also check for brick and mortar that is falling out or missing. Defects in the firebox usually can be repaired with refractory cement—a tough, heatproof sealant available through fireplace dealers. A damaged refractory liner in a prefabricated fireplace often can

be replaced without having to replace the entire unit.

Open the damper completely. It should move freely and sit snugly against the throat. Use a powerful flashlight to look up into the throat to check the condition of the damper. The damper should be sound with no cracks, severe pitting, or rusted-out sections. Over the years, however, a metal damper often will deteriorate from the water vapor and corrosive gases produced by the fireplace. Broken or corroded dampers should be replaced by a professional.

Look up inside the flue and check for broken or damaged brick or flue liner. Vertical cracking in the flue liner is a telltale sign of a previous flue fire. Any defects should be considered serious potential hazards. Consult a professional chimney sweep or a masonry contractor who is familiar with fireplace repairs *(see*

Relining a Chimney, page 148). Be prepared: Fixing or replacing a chimney liner is an expensive job.

Look for any obstructions such as branches or other debris that can restrict air flow. Finally, inspect for creosote deposits. If creosote has built up to a thickness greater than ⅛ inch, it should be removed.

If you can't see the entire flue from below, you'll have to get up on the roof and inspect the flue from the top of the chimney, something that can be quite dangerous to do, and you may wish to hire a professional chimney sweep to

Relining a Chimney, page 148).

Removing creosote from glass

Clean the glass doors on fireplaces, inserts, or wood stoves using a non-abrasive household window cleaner. Perform this chore only when the unit is completely cooled. Fireplace and wood stove specialty stores typically carry cleaning products made specifically for removing soot or creosote buildup from the inside surfaces of glass.

do this and to clean the chimney.

If you do decide to do this inspection yourself, don't climb up onto the roof unless your roof has a pitch of 6-in-12 or less, and unless you are completely confident of your abilities. Make a safety ladder by attaching ridge

hooks to the end of a ladder section. Use it by hanging the hooks over the roof ridge so the ladder lays flat and secure against the roof surface. Roof hooks are available at hardware stores and home improvement centers.

Fireplaces and Building Codes

For obvious reasons, the construction and installation of fireplaces and chimneys is strictly regulated by building codes and fire safety ordinances. This is true even if you are installing an insert and attaching it to an existing chimney. Most states require installations to be checked and approved by a building or fire safety official. An inspector looks for the following:

• The inside diameter of the chimney and flue liner and the cross-sectional area of the fireplace throat should have a minimum area of 50 square inches. A metal stovepipe 8 inches in diameter meets this requirement.

• There must be a minimum clearance between the exterior of the chimney and all combustible materials, typically 2 inches. Essentially, this makes a chimney freestanding—no wood framing members are attached to or even touch a chimney for its entire length. At the roof, where the chimney exits the house, the gap between the roof and the chimney typically is filled with nonflammable plaster and protected by metal flashing.

• The walls of a brick chimney must be at least 4 inches

thick. Chimney walls made of concrete block must be at least 12 inches thick.

• Masonry chimneys must be lined with a flue made of ⅝-inch-thick fireproof clay tile or 2-inch-thick firebrick, and all joints must be grouted with an approved, fireproof mortar. Metal flues must be code-approved, double-wall, insulated construction.

• Chimney height is dictated by local building codes. Typically, the chimney should terminate at least 2 feet above the highest point of the building that occurs within 10 feet of the chimney measured in any direction.

• Two appliances, such as a fireplace and a gas-burning stove, cannot be vented into the same chimney.

• Combustible materials surrounding a fireplace opening must allow 1 inch of clearance for each ⅛ inch they project out from the face of the fireplace, to a distance of 12 inches. For example, wood molding ¾ inch thick cannot be installed closer than 6 inches to the fireplace opening. Wood molding 1½ inches thick cannot be closer than 12 inches to the opening.

Chimneys: Inspecting and Cleaning

CLEANING A CHIMNEY IS NOT A difficult task for the homeowner, but common sense should prevail. You'll likely have to do this job from up on the roof, so take every precaution against accidents. Don't work on roofs with a pitch greater than 6-in-12. Wear good quality, rubber-soled shoes for traction. Use a safety ladder as described in *Inspecting Your Fireplace, page 151.* Even if you hire a chimney sweep, you'll want to know what needs to be done.

Always use the correct tools. Over the years, chimney cleaning has included a repertoire of homemade methods such as filling a burlap bag with rocks or chains, tying it to a rope, then lowering it down the flue to ream out dirt and deposits. Another method is to push a small pine or fire tree up and down inside the flue. Charming as these makeshift solutions may be, they risk damaging the interiors of flues, dislodging tiles, and creating potentially hazardous cracks.

The safest and most effective way to clean a chimney is with a chimney brush. These are usually big, round or square brushes with stiff wire or polypropylene bristles. These brushes are available at fireplace retailers and home improvement centers. Generally, the wire brushes cost more but are more effective and long-lasting than the plastic versions. The brushes are attached to long, flexible rods made of fiberglass. The rods have threaded ends so that additional rods can be added as needed. Tall chimneys may require several rods to reach from top to bottom.

The first step in chimney cleaning is to place a drop cloth in front of the fireplace to catch soot and debris. As an added precaution, seal off the front of the fireplace opening with a sheet of plastic and some duct tape. If you must tape the plastic to painted surfaces, use painter's tape. From the roof, the brush is pushed down into the flue, then another rod is screwed onto the assembly until the entire length of the flue is scrubbed clean. Then remove the plastic shield and clean the firebox with a scrub

brush. Use a heavy-duty shop vacuum for removing debris from the smoke shelf. Wear a respirator, safety goggles, gloves, and old clothes.

Special Considerations for Older Chimneys

The National Fire Protection Agency has required flue liners in all new chimneys since the early 1950s. Because older chimneys are not required to have liners, homeowners should be even more vigilant against defects that may cause fires. Regular inspection and cleaning is vital for continued safety.

There are two main areas of concern with unlined, all-brick chimneys. First, the mortar holding the bricks together may deteriorate over time, leaving gaps that provide conduits for heat or sparks to reach surrounding surfaces. Providing they can be reached, failing mortar joints can be repaired with refractory cement. Otherwise, the entire chimney may need to be relined *(see Relining a Chimney, page 148).*

The second concern is older construction techniques that didn't call for keeping a safe distance of 2 inches between masonry surfaces and wood framing members. Sometimes, masonry fireplaces were used to provide structural support for framing members. Attaching lumber to the outside of fireplace walls and building niches and shelves specifically to support key framing components was common chimney construction practice. Even though the outside portions of masonry chimney walls may never reach ignition temperatures of 450° F or hotter, wood that is too close to a chimney will undergo pyrolysis, a slow drying out and chemical change that eventually allows wood to ignite at temperatures as low as 200° F. The problem can occur if old lathe-and-plaster walls are positioned too close to chimneys, too. The solution is to examine the chimney closely along its entire length, from foundation to rooftop, for potential trouble spots, and to remove or reposition framing members or other flammable materials that are too close to chimney walls.

A thorough fireplace inspection and cleaning is a top-to-bottom affair.

• To prevent covering your nice clothes in soot, dress for the occasion. Wear goggles and a mask for protection. Plan to use a brush to remove all soot and debris loosened by cleaning the flue.

• Start by inspecting the firebox and damper to ensure there are no cracks in the masonry and that the flue is clear.

• Head up to the top of the chimney, and remove the cap to begin cleaning. Be sure to use the proper brushes to clean the flue.

• While you're up there, check the cap to be sure that it's still in good shape.

Chimneys: Exteriors

A CHIMNEY IS CONTINUALLY EXPOSED to the weather and changes in temperature. As a result, masonry materials, such as brick and mortar, can deteriorate. Weak or improperly mixed mortar can simply crumble over time. Moisture can penetrate cracks and fissures in masonry materials where it may freeze and expand, opening up gaps, cracking brick and stone, and causing mortar to fall out. In addition, water that gets inside a chimney can rust metal parts such as roof flashing, flue liners, and dampers, causing these parts to fail. Yearly inspections and preventative maintenance can prevent costly repairs.

To stop water damage, waterproof your chimney's exterior surfaces. Masonry, especially brick, is a porous material that readily absorbs water. Use a good-quality masonry sealer to keep moisture out. The best products are designed specifically to seal chimneys and are rated as "vapor permeable," meaning they will allow trapped moisture to escape but do not permit moisture to enter masonry from the outside. Do not use paint or other nonpermeable sealers—they may trap moisture inside the chimney and cause materials to deteriorate.

To prevent water from entering the chimney and causing the deterioration of interior masonry joints or metal components, install a chimney cap, also called a rain hat (*see page 131, Basic Components of a Fireplace*).

A rain hat should sit at least 12 inches above the end of the chimney opening. Rain hats usually are not required by code and not every chimney has one.

Other areas of chimney exteriors that may require care include:

Proper fireplace maintenance extends well outside the house—to the top of the chimney.

❧ *The chimney crown* is the top of a masonry chimney. It is made of concrete and is designed to cover and protect the uppermost edges of the chimney's parts, from the flue lining to the outer edges of the masonry veneer. Typically, the crown extends past the outer edges of a chimney 2 or 3 inches to afford the vertical chimney surfaces some protection from rain and sun. Because of its exposed position, the crown may suffer deterioration. The chances of failure increase because of the nature of concrete. Exposed to the extreme variations of heat and cold found at the top of a house, the crown expands and contracts, often resulting in hairline cracks. Once moisture enters these cracks, further deterioration is likely. It's important to have the crown inspected each year for any signs of cracking. Cracks should be patched with waterproof, non-shrinking concrete coatings available at hardware stores and home improvement centers.

➪ *Metal flashing* seals the joint between the chimney and the roof. It is designed to be integrated with roofing materials to prevent rain and melted snow from penetrating the roof system. The flashing should be inspected annually to check for signs of corrosion. Minor corrosion can be patched with asphalt roof sealant, available at hardware stores and home improvement centers. The sealant itself can crack and deteriorate over time and should be part of routine inspections. Badly corroded flashing should be replaced by a professional contractor.

Repairing Mortar Joints

Joints between brick or stone on chimney exteriors occasionally crack and fall out or crumble with age. To repair joints, they need to be "repointed," or "tuck-pointed." The process involves removing damaged mortar with a narrow cold chisel and a hammer to a depth of about ¼ inch, then "tucking" new mortar into the void with the point of a trowel. Use mortar repair mix, which has a latex binder additive. Clean out dust and particles with a shop vacuum, wet the joint with water to increase adhesion, then pack the new mortar into the joint. Finish the joint with the tip of a trowel to create a slight depression in the mortar, or use a "strike tool," a tool especially designed for creating even, smooth mortar joints. Remember that it is difficult to create an exact color match between the old mortar and the new.

Adequate protection at the vulnerable joint where chimney and roof meet ensures a watertight seal.

Safety and Insurance

BUILDING A FIRE INSIDE YOUR HOME requires common sense about safety. Keep in mind the following advice:

☞ *A fire extinguisher* can be handy for putting out small fires caused by errant sparks or a burning ember that falls onto the floor. Install a Class ABC fire extinguisher near the fireplace and make sure every member of your household knows its location and knows how to use it. In the event of a fire, there is little time for familiarizing yourself with the instructions. Most fireplace stores have small, decorative fire extinguisher storage units that can be installed in easy-to-reach locations near the fireplace.

Check the indicator monthly to make sure the unit is fully charged. Don't, however, let having a good fire extinguisher lull you into a false sense of security. And never underestimate a fire, no matter how small. Remember that fighting a fire is secondary to alerting all persons inside to evacuate the house and calling the fire department.

☞ *Install and maintain* smoke detectors according to the manufacturer's instructions. Your home should have one in each main living area, in each hallway, and outside bedrooms. Change batteries of battery-operated devices once each year.

☞ *Burn only firewood* in your fireplace or wood stove—never paper, pine boughs, or scraps of plywood or other "engineered" lumber. Hot pieces and ashes of these other materials can float out of your fireplace and cause a roof fire on your house or neighboring houses.

Carbon Monoxide

Carbon monoxide (CO) is an odorless, tasteless byproduct of combustion. Blocked vents or inefficient combustion in your furnace, water heater, or fireplace appliance can cause carbon monoxide to enter the home. Symptoms of exposure include headache, tiredness, and nausea. A battery-operated CO safety monitor, much like a smoke detector, emits a warning signal when it senses dangerous CO levels. These simple safety devices are available at home improvement centers and many other retailers.

☞ *Never leave a fire unattended.* If you must leave your home before the fire burns out, close glass doors or make sure a spark-arresting screen is placed in front of the fireplace opening. Do not use water to put out a fire; instead, smother fires with baking soda, sand, or cat litter.

☞ *When you decorate* the mantel, never have decorations below the upper surface of the mantelpiece. This is especially important during the winter holidays, when Christmas garlands or stockings are traditionally hung from the mantel. If you decorate your mantel this way, don't light a fire in the fireplace.

Insurance Issues

For the most part, an existing fireplace in a home is covered by a

standard homeowners' insurance policy. The exception may be free-standing fireplaces, such as wood-burning stoves. If you move into a home with a wood-burning stove, your agent may come to your home to inspect the unit.

If you plan to add a fireplace, change an existing fireplace, or install a wood-burning stove, be sure to call your insurance agent first. Your agent can also supply you with safety information about installing and using fireplaces and stoves.

Also check your insurance policy for coverage regarding the chimney. Much of the care chimneys is considered standard home maintenance, and

as such, if you have a problem, the repairs required may not be covered.

Words of Wisdom

When you purchase a fireplace or stove, be sure to read the manual and keep it handy. Every model is a bit different, and you'd be wise to know the particulars for safe and enjoyable operation. If the manual is lost or misplaced, be sure to contact the manufacturer for a new copy.

Seals of Approval

Every new fireplace or stove must have a Consumer Product Safety Commission (CPSC) label that gives you information about where to place the unit and how to use it. This label, however, does not ensure that the unit has been tested for safety.

Nationally recognized testing laboratories for wood-burning units are:

• Omni Environmental Services, Solid Fuel Testing Laboratory

• PFS Corporation

• Underwriters Laboratories, Inc.

• Underwriters Laboratories of Canada, Inc.

• Warnock Hersey International, Inc.

When buying a wood-burning unit, look for a seal from one of these sources to ensure that the unit meets minimum industry-accepted safety standards.

Snug and Safe

Think of fire safety and comfort when you're choosing and placing furnishings near the hearth.

• Always use a screen to keep flying embers under control.

• Except for flame-resistant hearth rugs, keep carpeting and area rugs away from the fireplace opening.

• Seating around the fire should be arranged with a clear view of the fire, but not so close that a wayward spark can land on fabric.

• For flexibility in design, consider a leather-covered, wheeled ottoman. It can be moved closer to the fire for those who want to get extra toasty, and moved near a chair as a foot prop when there's no fire.

NFPA #211

The standard bearer of installation requirements for solid-fuel burning devices—which include fireplaces and stoves—is the National Fire Protection Association (NFPA) Standard #211. Almost all manufacturers design their products to meet these specifications. Ask the dealer about compliance with NFPA before you buy a fireplace or stove, and be sure the unit is installed to this standard.

Resources

Fireplace Manufacturers

Aladdin Hearth Products
401 North Wynne St.
Colville, WA 99114
509/684-3745
www.aladdinhearth.com
Designer and manufacturer of
Quadra-Fire gas fireplaces and
Dovre gas, wood, and pellet stoves.

Alco-Brite
P.O. Box 840926
Hilldale, UT 84784
800/473-0717
www.alco-brite.com
Manufacturer of a combination of
gelled grape-ethanol alcohol related
products, including gel-burning
fireplace units, ceramic and refractory firelogs, and accessories.

Attika
c/o Rais & Wittus Inc.
23 Hack Green Rd.
Pound Ridge, NY 10576
914/764-5679
www.raiswittus.com
Manufacturer of Euro-style gas and
wood-burning stoves.

Austroflamm
c/o Austroflamm Handels GmbH
Gfereth 101
A-4631 Krenglbach
Austria
+43-7249-46443-0
www.austroflamm.com
Austrian manufacturer of Euro-style
wood and gas stoves.

Dimplex
1367 Industrial Rd.
Cambridge, Ontario, Canada N1R 7G8
800/668-6663
www.dimplex.com
Manufacturer of electric fireplaces
and stoves for the ambience of a
fire with no venting.

FireCraft Technologies
4325 Artesia Ave.
Fullerton, CA 92833
800/731-8101
800/232-1221
www.superiorfireplace.com
www.marcofireplace.com
Manufacturer of several major
hearth-product brands, including
Marco, Superior, Lennox Hearth,
Whitfield, and Security.

Fire Designs
1101 Isaac Shelby Dr.
Shelbyville, KY 40065
773/472-5014
Manufacturer of outdoor gel-fuel
patio fireplaces.

Fireplace Products International
6988 Venture St.
Delta, British Columbia,
Canada V4G 1H4
604/946-5155
www.regency-fire.com
www.waterfordstoves.com
Manufacturers of the Regency and
Waterford brands of stoves.

**Fireplace Manufacturers Inc.
(FMI)**
2701 South Harbor Blvd.
Santa Ana, CA 92704
714/549-7782
www.fmionline.com
Manufacturer of wood-burning and
gas-burning, vented and vent-free
fireplaces.

HearthStone
c/o HNC Inc.
Stafford Avenue P.O. Box 1069
Morrisville, VT 05661
800/827-8603, ext. 400
www.hearthstone.com
Producer of handmade soapstone
wood and gas stoves., each is
signed by the craftsperson who
made it.

Heatech
White River Junction, VT
802/295-8778
www.heatechstoves.com
Vermont-based hearth-product
maker of cast-iron stoves.

Heatilator
Division of Hearth Technologies Inc.
1915 West Saunders St.
Mt. Pleasant, IA 52641
800/843-2848
www.heatilator.com
This division of Hearth Technologies
Inc. produces a full range of
wood-burning and gas-burning
fireplaces.

Heat-N-Glo
20802 Kensington Blvd.
Lakeville, MN 55044
888/743-2887
www.heatnglo.com
This division of Hearth Technologies
makes a full line of gas-burning
fireplaces.

Jøtul
400 Riverside St.
P.O. Box 1157
Portland, ME 04104
207/797-5912
www.hearth.com/jotul/company.html
Manufacturer of gas-burning stoves.

Kozy Heat
800/253-4904
www.kozyheat.com
Manufacturer of both indoor and
patio gas-burning fireplaces.
Innovations include "bay window"
fire doors for 360-degree viewing.
Also offers a wood-burning unit that
can be converted to gas.

**Majestic Fireplaces/Vermont
Castings**
1000 East Market St.
Huntington, IN 46750
800/227-8683
www.majesticproducts.com
Manufacturer of wood-burning and
gas-burning fireplaces and stoves;
hearth systems; and accessories.

Malm
368 Yolanda Ave.
Santa Rosa, CA 95404
800/535-8955
www.malmfireplaces.com
Manufacturer of gas- and wood-
burning fireplaces and the FireFlame
wood-burning fireplace-BBQ grill. Also
custom-designs fireplaces.

Pacific Energy
P.O. Box 1060
Duncan, British Columbia
Canada V9L 3Y2
250/748-1184
www.pacificenergy.bc.ca
Wood and gas stoves and inserts.

Rais
C/O Rais & Wittus Inc.
23 Hack Green Rd.
Pound Ridge, NY 10576
914/764-5679
www.raiswittus.com
Euro-style high-efficiency stoves.

Real Flame/Jensen Company Store
c/o The Jensen Company
7800 Northwestern Ave.
Racine, WI 53406
800/654-1704
www.realflame.com
Manufacturer of gel fuels, gel-burning fireplace units, and mantels,
and accessories.

Robert H. Peterson Company
14724 E. Proctor Ave.
City of Industry, CA 91746
800/332-0240
www.rhpeterson.com
Manufacturer of gas logs.

RSF Energy
c/o Industrial Chimney Co./RSF
Energy
801 St. Nicholas
St. Jerome, Quebec, Canada J7Y 4C7
450/565-6336
www.icc-rsf.com
Manufacturer specializing in high-
tech, high-efficiency, clean-burning
wood hearth products.

Sunsor Products
2801 Carlisle Ave.
Racine, WI 53404
800/776-6966
www.sunsorproducts.com
Manufacturer of gel fuels and gel-
fuel fireplaces, and ceramic logs.

Thelin
800/949-5048
www.thelinco.com
Manufacturer of pellet and gas stoves
with an old-time, pot-belly look.

Travis Industries, Inc.
10850 117th Place NE
Kirkland, WA 98033
425/827-9505
www.hearth.com/travis
Manufacturer of Lopi brand wood,
pellet, and gas stoves and fireplace
inserts; Fireplace Xtraordinair wood
and gas fireplaces and inserts; and
Avalon wood, pellet, and gas stoves
and inserts.

Tulikivi U.S. Inc.
250 West 34th St., Ste. 3600
New York, NY 10119
800/843-3473
www.tulikivi.com
Tulikivi is Finnish for "fire stone".
The company makes wood-burning
soapstone fireplaces that cleanly
and efficiently absorb and radiate
heat into the room.

Vestal Fires Inc.
P.O. Box 307
Manhattan, IL 60442
815/423-5018
www.vestalfires.com
Manufactures ventless alcohol-
based, gel-fuel-burning fireplaces
and accessories.

Virtual Fireplaces
www.virtualproducts.com
Specialized high-definition digital
monitor that fits into existing
fireplace cavity or into new
construction to provide the image
and sound of wood-burning fire.
Kick-plate heater is available. Sold
via Internet only.

Whitfield Hearth Products
695 Pease Rd.
Burlington, WA 98233
360/757-9728
www.whitfield.com
Manufacturer of pellet and gas
stoves and inserts.

Wilkening Fireplace Co.
9608 State 371 N.W.
Walker, MN 56484
800/367-7967
www.hearth.com/wilkening/info.html
Manufacturer of high-efficiency
wood-burning fireplaces featuring
the Ultimate Seal airtight door,
including the Intens-A-Fyre, Ultra
Great, and Magna-Fyre.

Woodstock Soapstone Co. Inc.
66 Airpark Rd.
West Lebanon, NH 03784
800/866-4344
www.woodstocksoapstone.com
Woodstock handmade wood and
gas-burning stoves, including a
catalytic wood stove, with the even,
radiant heat of soapstone.

Mantel & Surround Suppliers

A+ Woodworking
P.O. Box 116
Cleveland, SC 29635-0116
864/836-2918
www.custommantels.com
Manufacturer of custom mantels,
shelves, and mantel ornaments

Architectural Salvage Warehouse
212 Battery St.
Burlington, VT 05401
802/658-5011
www.architecturalsalvagevt.com
Antiques warehouse carrying
salvaged mantels.

Carolina Architectural Salvage
110 S. Palmer St.
Ridgeway, SC 29130
803/337-3939
Salvaged hearth items.

Carroll's Mantels
417 CR 135
Troy, AL 36079
334/735-3217
www.carrollmantels.com
Custom-built mantel manufacturer.

Collinswood Designs
1400 Duff Dr.
Fort Collins, CO 80524
800/626-8357
www.collinswooddesigns.com
Shelves, surrounds, related
cabinetry, overmantels. Factory-
direct sales.

Danny Alessandro Ltd.
223 E. 59th St.
New York, NY 10022
212/421-1928
www.alessandroltd.com
Antique mantels and
accoutrements, with emphasis on
18th- and 19th-century French;
English and American antique
pieces also available.

**Designer Fireplace Mantels and
Ornamental Architecture**
610/313-1821
www.designer-fireplace-
mantles.com
Custom mantels of cast plaster,
cast stone, GFRG, and GFRC can be
finished to simulate stone, and
accept paint and gilding .

Designer Stencils
3634 Silverside Rd.
Wilmington, DE 19810
800/822-7838
www.designerstencils.com
Complete stencils for creating a
faux fireplace.

Distinctive Mantel Designs
555 Santa Fe Dr.
Denver, CO 80204
303/592-7474
www.asgusa.com
Maker of wood and cast-stone
mantels.

Elegance in Stone
www.eleganceinstone.com
Fireplace surrounds of granite,
marble, and limestone.

Living Wood Industries
4325 Chippewa Ln.
Maple Plain, MN 55359
612/476-4081
www.livingwood.com
Creates mantel surrounds in a
variety of styles; sold in kits with
complete installation instructions.

Old World Stoneworks
5400 Miller Ave.
Dallas, TX 75206
800/600-8336
www.oldstoneworks.com
Cast-stone mantels and surrounds.

Salvage One
1524 S. Sangamon St.
Chicago, IL 60608
312/733-0098
www.salvageone.com
Large architectural salvage
warehouse that sells surrounds,
mantels, and firebacks.

Woodmaster
800/285-8551
Hand-crafted mantels, shelves, and
mantel caps.

Associations

**Chimney Safety Institute of
America**
8752 Robbins Rd.
Indianapolis, IN 46268
800/536-0118
www.csia.org
Call or use the website to find CSIA
certified sweeps in your area.

**Gas Appliance Manufacturers
Association**
1901 N. Moore St.
Arlington, VA 22209
703/525-9565
www.gamanet.org

Hearth Education Foundation
65 Harvester Ave.
Batavia, NY 14020
716/343-6524
www.hearthed.com
Use the website to find local HEF-
certified professionals.

Hearth Products Association
1601 N. Kent St., Ste 1001
Arlington, VA 22209
703/522-0086
www.hearthassoc.org

**Masonry Heater Association of
North America**
RR2 Box 33M
Randolf, VT 05060
802/728-5896
www.mha-net.clever.net
Use the website to find a local
certified heater mason.

National Chimney Sweep Guild
www.ncsg.org
Also see listing for Chimney Safety
Institute of America.

**National Fire Protection
Association**
1 Batterymarch Park
P.O. Box 9101
Quincy, MA 02269
800/344-3555
www.nfpa.org
This organization provides helpful
consumer safety information.

Pellet Fuels Institute
1601 N. Kent St., Ste. 1001
Arlington, VA 22209
888/287-3167
www.pelletheat.org

Buckley Rumford Fireplaces
1035 Monroe St.
Port Townsend, WA 98368

Index

Numbers in **bold italics** indicate photographs of the subject.

CONTRIBUTING PHOTOGRAPHERS:

Page 85, candles; page 127, outdoor gel-fueled fireplace; page 136, andirons: Scott Little, Primary Image
Page 101, stone fireplace; page 137, copper kettle: Peter Krumhardt

Thanks to the manufacturers listed for the photos used on the following pages:

Page 119: Jøtul
Page 120: Rais
Page 121: Tulikivi
Page 123: Dimplex
Page 125: Designer Stencils
Page 127: Top, Huntington. Bottom, Fire Designs
Page 128: Majestic
Page 130: Majestic
Page 140: Theilen
Page 141: Majestic
Page 144: Robert H. Peterson Company
Page 146: Pellet Fuels Institute
Page 147: Majestic

To contact these manufacturers, please refer to Resources, pages 158-159.